# MVNO
# Complete Self-Assessment Guide

The guidance in this Self-Assessment is based on MVNO best practices and standards in business process architecture, design and quality management. The guidance is also based on the professional judgment of the individual collaborators listed in the Acknowledgments.

**Notice of rights**

Copyright © by The Art of Service
http://theartofservice.com
service@theartofservice.com

# Table of Contents

# About The Art of Service

The Art of Service, Business Process Architects since 2000, is dedicated to helping stakeholders achieve excellence.

Defining, designing, creating, and implementing a process to solve a stakeholders challenge or meet an objective is the most valuable role… In EVERY group, company, organization and department.

Unless you're talking a one-time, single-use project, there should be a process. Whether that process is managed and implemented by humans, AI, or a combination of the two, it needs to be designed by someone with a complex enough perspective to ask the right questions.

Someone capable of asking the right questions and step back and say, 'What are we really trying to accomplish here? And is there a different way to look at it?'

With The Art of Service's Standard Requirements Self-Assessments, we empower people who can do just that — whether their title is marketer, entrepreneur, manager, salesperson, consultant, Business Process Manager, executive assistant, IT Manager, CIO etc... —they are the people who rule the future. They are people who watch the process as it happens, and ask the right questions to make the process work better.

**Contact us when you need any support with this Self-Assessment and any help with templates, blue-prints and examples of standard documents you might need:**

http://theartofservice.com
service@theartofservice.com

# Acknowledgments

This checklist was developed under the auspices of The Art of Service, chaired by Gerardus Blokdyk.

Representatives from several client companies participated in the preparation of this Self-Assessment.

In addition, we are thankful for the design and printing services provided.

# Included Resources - how to access

Included with your purchase of the book is the MVNO Self-Assessment Spreadsheet Dashboard which contains all questions and Self-Assessment areas and auto-generates insights, graphs, and project RACI planning - all with examples to get you started right away.

How? Simply send an email to
**access@theartofservice.com**
with this books' title in the subject to get the MVNO Self Assessment Tool right away.

You will receive the following contents with New and Updated specific criteria:

•    The latest quick edition of the book in PDF

•    The latest complete edition of the book in PDF, which criteria correspond to the criteria in...

•    The Self-Assessment Excel Dashboard, and...

•    Example pre-filled Self-Assessment Excel Dashboard to get familiar with results generation

•    In-depth specific Checklists covering the topic

•    Project management checklists and templates to assist with implementation

**INCLUDES LIFETIME SELF ASSESSMENT UPDATES**

Every self assessment comes with Lifetime Updates and Lifetime Free Updated Books. Lifetime Updates is an industry-first feature which allows you to receive verified self assessment updates, ensuring you always have the most accurate information at your fingertips.

Get it now- you will be glad you did - do it now, before you forget.

Send an email to **access@theartofservice.com** with this books' title in the subject to get the MVNO Self Assessment Tool right away.

# Your feedback is invaluable to us

If you recently bought this book, we would love to hear from you! You can do this by writing a review on amazon (or the online store where you purchased this book) about your last purchase! As part of our continual service improvement process, we love to hear real client experiences and feedback.

### How does it work?
To post a review on Amazon, just log in to your account and click on the Create Your Own Review button (under Customer Reviews) of the relevant product page. You can find examples of product reviews in Amazon. If you purchased from another online store, simply follow their procedures.

### What happens when I submit my review?
Once you have submitted your review, send us an email at review@theartofservice.com with the link to your review so we can properly thank you for your feedback.

# Purpose of this Self-Assessment

This Self-Assessment has been developed to improve understanding of the requirements and elements of MVNO, based on best practices and standards in business process architecture, design and quality management.

It is designed to allow for a rapid Self-Assessment to determine how closely existing management practices and procedures correspond to the elements of the Self-Assessment.

The criteria of requirements and elements of MVNO have been rephrased in the format of a Self-Assessment questionnaire, with a seven-criterion scoring system, as explained in this document.

In this format, even with limited background knowledge of MVNO, a manager can quickly review existing operations to determine how they measure up to the standards. This in turn can serve as the starting point of a 'gap analysis' to identify management tools or system elements that might usefully be implemented in the organization to help improve overall performance.

# How to use the Self-Assessment

On the following pages are a series of questions to identify to what extent your MVNO initiative is complete in comparison to the requirements set in standards.

To facilitate answering the questions, there is a space in front of each question to enter a score on a scale of '1' to '5'.

1 Strongly Disagree

2 Disagree

3 Neutral

4 Agree

5 Strongly Agree

*Read the question and rate it with the following in front of mind:*

## 'In my belief,
## the answer to this question is clearly defined'.

There are two ways in which you can choose to interpret this statement;
1. how aware are you that the answer to the question is clearly defined
2. for more in-depth analysis you can choose to gather evidence and confirm the answer to the question. This obviously will take more time, most Self-Assessment

users opt for the first way to interpret the question and dig deeper later on based on the outcome of the overall Self-Assessment.

A score of '1' would mean that the answer is not clear at all, where a '5' would mean the answer is crystal clear and defined. Leave emtpy when the question is not applicable or you don't want to answer it, you can skip it without affecting your score. Write your score in the space provided.

After you have responded to all the appropriate statements in each section, compute your average score for that section, using the formula provided, and round to the nearest tenth. Then transfer to the corresponding spoke in the MVNO Scorecard on the second next page of the Self-Assessment.

Your completed MVNO Scorecard will give you a clear presentation of which MVNO areas need attention.

# MVNO
# Scorecard Example

Example of how the finalized Scorecard can look like:

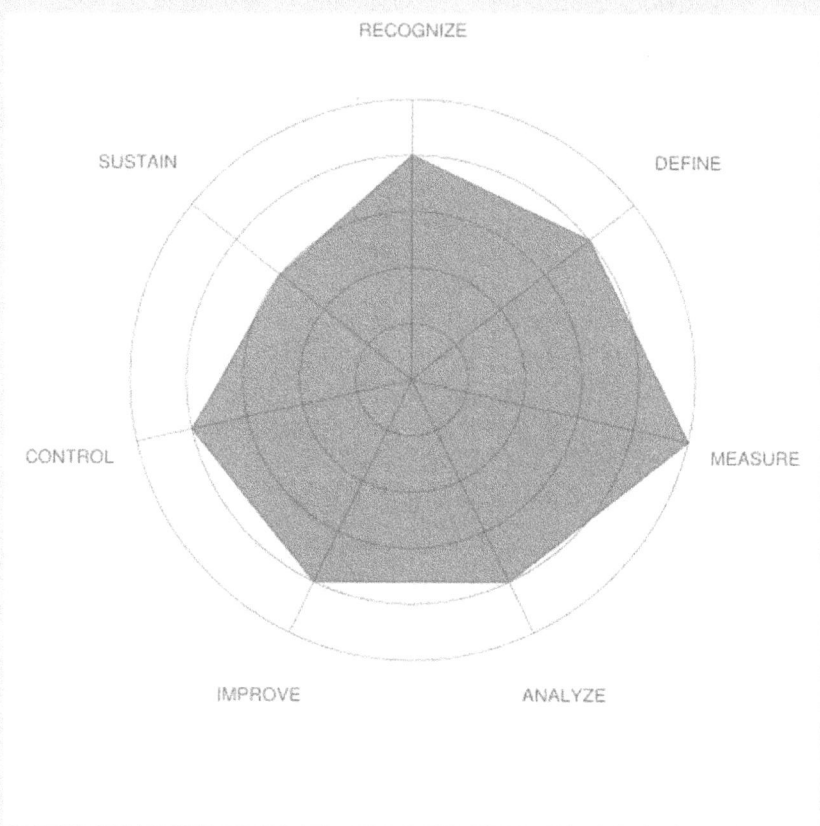

# MVNO
# Scorecard

Your Scores:

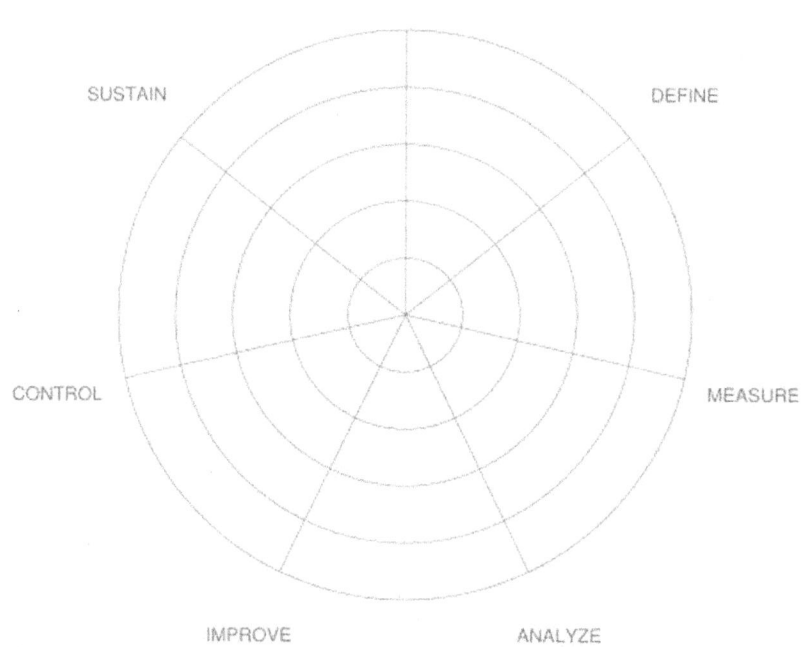

# BEGINNING OF THE SELF-ASSESSMENT:

# CRITERION #1: RECOGNIZE

INTENT: Be aware of the need for change. Recognize that there is an unfavorable variation, problem or symptom.

In my belief, the answer to this question is clearly defined:

5 Strongly Agree

4 Agree

3 Neutral

2 Disagree

1 Strongly Disagree

1. Who are your key stakeholders who need to sign off?
<--- Score

2. What is the MVNO problem definition? What do you need to resolve?
<--- Score

3. Does MVNO create potential expectations in other

areas that need to be recognized and considered?
<--- Score

**4. Is there a need to change the structure based on your organizations organizational and leadership life cycle?**
<--- Score

5. What is the problem or issue?
<--- Score

**6. Why do you need MVNOs?**
<--- Score

**7. Where will the carrier get the revenue needed to invest in the network?**
<--- Score

**8. What will the customer satisfaction entail, that is, what are the needs I am trying to meet?**
<--- Score

**9. How much bandwidth do you need?**
<--- Score

10. How do you identify the kinds of information that you will need?
<--- Score

**11. What will the customer satisfaction entail, that is, what are the needs you are trying to meet?**
<--- Score

12. What problems are you facing and how do you consider MVNO will circumvent those obstacles?
<--- Score

13. To what extent would your organization benefit from being recognized as a award recipient?
<--- Score

**14. Are you acquiring the talent you need?**
<--- Score

15. As a sponsor, customer or management, how important is it to meet goals, objectives?
<--- Score

16. What does MVNO success mean to the stakeholders?
<--- Score

17. Do you have/need 24-hour access to key personnel?
<--- Score

18. Are employees recognized or rewarded for performance that demonstrates the highest levels of integrity?
<--- Score

**19. With regard to stakeholder retention, what needs does your organization have in terms of supports, resources, and unanswered questions?**
<--- Score

**20. What tools will you need?**
<--- Score

**21. Do roaming agreements resolve your coverage issues?**
<--- Score

**22. Does the current or future labor market indicate the appropriate availability of talent needed for your organization to stay competitive?**
<--- Score

23. Have you identified your MVNO key performance indicators?
<--- Score

24. Will it solve real problems?
<--- Score

25. What else needs to be measured?
<--- Score

26. What are the expected benefits of MVNO to the stakeholder?
<--- Score

27. What situation(s) led to this MVNO Self Assessment?
<--- Score

**28. What type of license should be issued to an MVNO?**
<--- Score

29. Are there any specific expectations or concerns about the MVNO team, MVNO itself?
<--- Score

**30. Have the employee and customer satisfaction issues been picked up?**
<--- Score

31. How are you going to measure success?
<--- Score

**32. Should MVNO access to MNO networks be prevented?**
<--- Score

33. What should be considered when identifying available resources, constraints, and deadlines?
<--- Score

34. For your MVNO project, identify and describe the business environment, is there more than one layer to the business environment?
<--- Score

35. What would happen if MVNO weren't done?
<--- Score

36. What extra resources will you need?
<--- Score

37. How are the MVNO's objectives aligned to the group's overall stakeholder strategy?
<--- Score

**38. Do you have the needed human talent to meet the requirements?**
<--- Score

**39. Do you have a backlog of legacy integration needs creating bottlenecks on your path to better customer satisfaction and greater operational efficiency?**
<--- Score

**40. Are there any CDR retention requirements to consider including time they need to be stored?**
<--- Score

**41. What are the key issues and trends?**
<--- Score

**42. Have you identified the resources needed to ensure that customers needs are being met and to help enhance customer satisfaction?**
<--- Score

43. Who needs to know about MVNO?
<--- Score

**44. Where do you find the talent you need?**
<--- Score

45. What needs to be done?
<--- Score

46. Will a response program recognize when a crisis occurs and provide some level of response?
<--- Score

**47. How many devices do you need to keep online?**
<--- Score

48. How much are sponsors, customers, partners, stakeholders involved in MVNO? In other words, what are the risks, if MVNO does not deliver successfully?
<--- Score

**49. How do you identify critical talent segments?**
<--- Score

**50. What are the systemic issues that complicate and or undermine the retention of stakeholders?**
<--- Score

**51. How prepared is your organization to address issues related to talent attraction and retention in the next five years?**
<--- Score

**52. What type of talent do you need, and how much?**
<--- Score

**53. What type of talent do you need to attract and who to select?**
<--- Score

54. Who else hopes to benefit from it?
<--- Score

**55. Do customers and employees report the same kinds of events and behaviors leading to satisfaction and dissatisfaction in service encounters?**
<--- Score

56. What are the stakeholder objectives to be achieved with MVNO?
<--- Score

**57. Does your service ensure timely access to high quality talent that meets customer needs?**
<--- Score

**58. What expertise will you need?**
<--- Score

**59. What types of talent do you need across your businesses and geographies and where are demographic shifts creating gaps in your supply-demand forecast?**

<--- Score

**60. If this is what you need, now, how much of that resides within your current talent base?**

<--- Score

61. Should you invest in industry-recognized qualifications?

<--- Score

62. Are controls defined to recognize and contain problems?

<--- Score

Add up total points for this section:

_ _ _ _ _ = Total points for this section

Divided by: _ _ _ _ _ _ (number of statements answered) = _ _ _ _ _ _

Average score for this section

Transfer your score to the MVNO Index at the beginning of the Self-Assessment.

# CRITERION #2: DEFINE:

INTENT: Formulate the stakeholder problem. Define the problem, needs and objectives.

In my belief, the answer to this question is clearly defined:

5 Strongly Agree

4 Agree

3 Neutral

2 Disagree

1 Strongly Disagree

1. Have the customer needs been translated into specific, measurable requirements? How?
<--- Score

2. What key stakeholder process output measure(s) does MVNO leverage and how?
<--- Score

3. How does the MVNO manager ensure against scope

creep?
<--- Score

4. What are the compelling stakeholder reasons for embarking on MVNO?
<--- Score

5. Is the current 'as is' process being followed? If not, what are the discrepancies?
<--- Score

6. How would you define MVNO leadership?
<--- Score

7. What critical content must be communicated – who, what, when, where, and how?
<--- Score

8. Has a team charter been developed and communicated?
<--- Score

9. How was the 'as is' process map developed, reviewed, verified and validated?
<--- Score

10. Is full participation by members in regularly held team meetings guaranteed?
<--- Score

11. Is there regularly 100% attendance at the team meetings? If not, have appointed substitutes attended to preserve cross-functionality and full representation?
<--- Score

12. How do you gather the stories?
<--- Score

13. Who are the MVNO improvement team members, including Management Leads and Coaches?
<--- Score

14. Is a fully trained team formed, supported, and committed to work on the MVNO improvements?
<--- Score

15. What scope to assess?
<--- Score

**16. What key positions and talent requirements are likely to emerge in your organization s future?**
<--- Score

17. Is MVNO required?
<--- Score

18. When is the estimated completion date?
<--- Score

**19. How do your commercial mobile networks meet mission-critical requirements?**
<--- Score

20. What are the boundaries of the scope? What is in bounds and what is not? What is the start point? What is the stop point?
<--- Score

21. Will team members regularly document their MVNO work?
<--- Score

22. How do you keep key subject matter experts in the loop?
<--- Score

23. Is the team formed and are team leaders (Coaches and Management Leads) assigned?
<--- Score

24. When is/was the MVNO start date?
<--- Score

25. How can the value of MVNO be defined?
<--- Score

26. Has the MVNO work been fairly and/or equitably divided and delegated among team members who are qualified and capable to perform the work? Has everyone contributed?
<--- Score

27. Are different versions of process maps needed to account for the different types of inputs?
<--- Score

**28. Should the national wireless carriers be required to make available a certain amount of capacity on networks for MVNOs to use at commercially negotiated rates?**
<--- Score

29. How often are the team meetings?
<--- Score

**30. What are the boundaries of servant leadership in your organization. For example, are there**

**certain types of situations or contexts in which servant leader characteristics flourish?**
<--- Score

31. Is MVNO currently on schedule according to the plan?
<--- Score

32. What are the MVNO tasks and definitions?
<--- Score

33. Is MVNO linked to key stakeholder goals and objectives?
<--- Score

34. What are the rough order estimates on cost savings/opportunities that MVNO brings?
<--- Score

35. How do you gather requirements?
<--- Score

36. What constraints exist that might impact the team?
<--- Score

37. Do the problem and goal statements meet the SMART criteria (specific, measurable, attainable, relevant, and time-bound)?
<--- Score

38. How will the MVNO team and the group measure complete success of MVNO?
<--- Score

39. How did the MVNO manager receive input to the

development of a MVNO improvement plan and the estimated completion dates/times of each activity?
<--- Score

40. What would be the goal or target for a MVNO's improvement team?
<--- Score

41. Are team charters developed?
<--- Score

42. What are the dynamics of the communication plan?
<--- Score

43. Are there any constraints known that bear on the ability to perform MVNO work? How is the team addressing them?
<--- Score

44. What is the scope of the MVNO effort?
<--- Score

45. What are the Roles and Responsibilities for each team member and its leadership? Where is this documented?
<--- Score

46. Is the MVNO scope manageable?
<--- Score

47. Has the direction changed at all during the course of MVNO? If so, when did it change and why?
<--- Score

48. How do you think the partners involved in MVNO

would have defined success?
<--- Score

49. Are improvement team members fully trained on MVNO?
<--- Score

50. Has a project plan, Gantt chart, or similar been developed/completed?
<--- Score

**51. What consumer requirements does it address?**
<--- Score

52. Is there a MVNO management charter, including stakeholder case, problem and goal statements, scope, milestones, roles and responsibilities, communication plan?
<--- Score

53. Is the team adequately staffed with the desired cross-functionality? If not, what additional resources are available to the team?
<--- Score

**54. What are the auditing requirements for your contractors partners/subcontractors?**
<--- Score

55. What are the record-keeping requirements of MVNO activities?
<--- Score

56. Has everyone on the team, including the team leaders, been properly trained?
<--- Score

57. Are there different segments of customers?
<--- Score

58. Is there a critical path to deliver MVNO results?
<--- Score

59. Are customers identified and high impact areas defined?
<--- Score

60. Has anyone else (internal or external to the group) attempted to solve this problem or a similar one before? If so, what knowledge can be leveraged from these previous efforts?
<--- Score

61. What defines best in class?
<--- Score

**62. What kind of voice calls require acquisition of termination access by the originating network?**
<--- Score

63. Is it clearly defined in and to your organization what you do?
<--- Score

64. How do you hand over MVNO context?
<--- Score

65. Is data collected and displayed to better understand customer(s) critical needs and requirements.
<--- Score

66. How will variation in the actual durations of each activity be dealt with to ensure that the expected MVNO results are met?
<--- Score

67. Has/have the customer(s) been identified?
<--- Score

68. Have all basic functions of MVNO been defined?
<--- Score

69. Does the team have regular meetings?
<--- Score

70. Will team members perform MVNO work when assigned and in a timely fashion?
<--- Score

71. Is special MVNO user knowledge required?
<--- Score

**72. Does top management ensure that customer requirements are determined and met with the goal to achieve customer satisfaction?**
<--- Score

**73. Will changes in roaming regulation (ie roam like you are at home) unhinge the business case for the roaming MVNOs?**
<--- Score

74. Is the MVNO scope complete and appropriately sized?
<--- Score

**75. If you are launching a new MVNO, have you**

**modelled the business case to a granular enough level?**
<--- Score

76. What sort of initial information to gather?
<--- Score

77. When are meeting minutes sent out? Who is on the distribution list?
<--- Score

78. In what way can you redefine the criteria of choice clients have in your category in your favor?
<--- Score

79. Is the improvement team aware of the different versions of a process: what they think it is vs. what it actually is vs. what it should be vs. what it could be?
<--- Score

80. What specifically is the problem? Where does it occur? When does it occur? What is its extent?
<--- Score

81. Are accountability and ownership for MVNO clearly defined?
<--- Score

82. Is the team equipped with available and reliable resources?
<--- Score

83. Are customer(s) identified and segmented according to their different needs and requirements?
<--- Score

**84. How do the price agreements affect your business case as a MVNO?**
<--- Score

85. Have specific policy objectives been defined?
<--- Score

86. Are stakeholder processes mapped?
<--- Score

87. Are resources adequate for the scope?
<--- Score

88. What is out of scope?
<--- Score

89. Has the improvement team collected the 'voice of the customer' (obtained feedback – qualitative and quantitative)?
<--- Score

90. How is the team tracking and documenting its work?
<--- Score

91. Is the team sponsored by a champion or stakeholder leader?
<--- Score

92. Is there a completed, verified, and validated high-level 'as is' (not 'should be' or 'could be') stakeholder process map?
<--- Score

93. If substitutes have been appointed, have they been briefed on the MVNO goals and received regular

communications as to the progress to date?
<--- Score

94. Has a high-level 'as is' process map been completed, verified and validated?
<--- Score

95. What baselines are required to be defined and managed?
<--- Score

96. What customer feedback methods were used to solicit their input?
<--- Score

97. Is there a completed SIPOC representation, describing the Suppliers, Inputs, Process, Outputs, and Customers?
<--- Score

Add up total points for this section:
_ _ _ _ _  = Total points for this section

Divided by: _ _ _ _ _ _ (number of
statements answered) = _ _ _ _ _ _
Average score for this section

Transfer your score to the MVNO
Index at the beginning of the Self-
Assessment.

# CRITERION #3: MEASURE:

INTENT: Gather the correct data. Measure the current performance and evolution of the situation.

In my belief, the answer to this question is clearly defined:

5 Strongly Agree

4 Agree

3 Neutral

2 Disagree

1 Strongly Disagree

1. Is there an opportunity to verify requirements?
<--- Score

**2. What impacts future retention of employees at your organization?**
<--- Score

**3. What capabilities does your organization need to be effective with workforce analytics?**

<--- Score

**4. What types of problems is your organization attempting to solve with workforce analytics?**
<--- Score

**5. What are the benefits of people analytics?**
<--- Score

**6. How do you measure customer/stakeholder satisfaction?**
<--- Score

**7. Does your organization recognize the value of analytically driven insight?**
<--- Score

**8. Do you track measures of customer satisfaction related to quality delivery, etc.?**
<--- Score

9. Was a business case (cost/benefit) developed?
<--- Score

**10. How is workforce analytics aligned to the business objectives of your organization?**
<--- Score

11. Why do the measurements/indicators matter?
<--- Score

12. How are you verifying it?
<--- Score

**13. What types of business challenges are you able to address using people analytics?**

<--- Score

14. How is performance measured?
<--- Score

15. How is the value delivered by MVNO being measured?
<--- Score

16. What methods are feasible and acceptable to estimate the impact of reforms?
<--- Score

**17. How is the growth in data traffic impacting MVNOs?**
<--- Score

**18. Does it significantly impact customer satisfaction?**
<--- Score

**19. What significantly impacts customer satisfaction?**
<--- Score

**20. How do you transition to more advanced analytics capabilities?**
<--- Score

**21. How is ipv6 transition done in practice and what issues does it cause?**
<--- Score

**22. What will it take to make the case to use analytics to solve problems?**
<--- Score

23. Do you aggressively reward and promote the people who have the biggest impact on creating excellent MVNO services/products?
<--- Score

**24. How do you manage the fluidity of the analytics process and the fact there is not a perfect state?**
<--- Score

25. Have you made assumptions about the shape of the future, particularly its impact on your customers and competitors?
<--- Score

**26. What is your data that suggests that analytics is critical for the future?**
<--- Score

**27. Low costs for educated talent was a motivation for offshoring. Now, however, is demand exceeding supply?**
<--- Score

**28. Do your organizations processes explicitly accommodate analytics?**
<--- Score

**29. Retrospective analysis: what have you done?**
<--- Score

30. Have design-to-cost goals been established?
<--- Score

**31. How effective is your organization at using**

**data and analytics to make talent decisions?**
<--- Score

**32. What should your organization look like to support the reporting and analytics needs of stakeholders?**
<--- Score

**33. How does your organization deploy analytics to improve strategy execution and business performance?**
<--- Score

34. How do you verify and develop ideas and innovations?
<--- Score

**35. Is the cost of subscribing to any mobile phone network prohibitive?**
<--- Score

36. How will your organization measure success?
<--- Score

**37. What is the purpose of workforce analytics in your organization?**
<--- Score

**38. Is there a focus on customer needs and customer satisfaction in your unit or team?**
<--- Score

**39. What area do you see analytics most readily being applied to in your organization?**
<--- Score

40. What is an unallowable cost?
<--- Score

41. Are the MVNO benefits worth its costs?
<--- Score

42. Did you tackle the cause or the symptom?
<--- Score

**43. How do you hire, retain, communicate and organize your analytic talent?**
<--- Score

44. How do you focus on what is right -not who is right?
<--- Score

45. Who should receive measurement reports?
<--- Score

46. What causes innovation to fail or succeed in your organization?
<--- Score

**47. What are the stages of your Talent Acquisition Analytics Funnel?**
<--- Score

**48. How do you get funding to build your talent analytics capabilities?**
<--- Score

**49. How do switching costs moderate the effect of customer satisfaction and perceived value on customer loyalty?**
<--- Score

**50. What skills and competencies are required for the development of effective workforce analytics?**
<--- Score

51. How are measurements made?
<--- Score

52. What could cause you to change course?
<--- Score

**53. What data do you have to get key analytics?**
<--- Score

**54. What would you like to explore through analytics that you are unable to do today?**
<--- Score

**55. Where are you (and where do you need to be) in developing your analytics competency?**
<--- Score

56. How will success or failure be measured?
<--- Score

**57. What is the Network Cost/line?**
<--- Score

58. Do you have any cost MVNO limitation requirements?
<--- Score

59. What are the MVNO key cost drivers?
<--- Score

**60. How can your MNO/MVNO refocus on customer**

**volumes and reduce churn better?**
<--- Score

**61. Where should you focus talent analytics?**
<--- Score

62. When are costs are incurred?
<--- Score

63. How do you control the overall costs of your work processes?
<--- Score

**64. Performance Standard: What should be the standards for completeness, reliability, accuracy, timeliness, customer satisfaction, quality and/or cost?**
<--- Score

**65. How do you get leadership support for talent analytics?**
<--- Score

**66. What are the challenges of viewing and analysing large amounts of user-provided data?**
<--- Score

67. How will costs be allocated?
<--- Score

68. Will MVNO have an impact on current business continuity, disaster recovery processes and/or infrastructure?
<--- Score

69. Why do you expend time and effort to implement

measurement, for whom?
<--- Score

**70. What kind of organization and specific skills are needed to support your organizations analytics capability?**
<--- Score

71. Has a cost center been established?
<--- Score

72. How do you verify performance?
<--- Score

**73. How do you develop a market analysis/ business case?**
<--- Score

**74. What barriers do you face with regards to talent analytics within your organization?**
<--- Score

**75. What metrics do you use to measure the linkage between customer satisfaction and customer loyalty?**
<--- Score

76. What is your MVNO quality cost segregation study?
<--- Score

77. What tests verify requirements?
<--- Score

78. Are there competing MVNO priorities?
<--- Score

**79. Why should your organization invest in people analytics today?**
<--- Score

**80. Is customer satisfaction measured?**
<--- Score

**81. How do you measure engagement?**
<--- Score

**82. What is the cause of actual performance?**
<--- Score

**83. What are your performance levels and trends for the key measures of customer satisfaction?**
<--- Score

**84. What do you measure about your workforce?**
<--- Score

85. How will you measure your MVNO effectiveness?
<--- Score

**86. What social and unstructured data do you currently gather and how do you analyze it?**
<--- Score

87. How will effects be measured?
<--- Score

88. What potential environmental factors impact the MVNO effort?
<--- Score

**89. Does workforce analytics deliver a holistic**

**understanding of your employees and enable you to focus more on strategy, less on data manipulation?**

<--- Score

**90. What will be the full cost of building a full municipal network?**

<--- Score

**91. Does this system also allow you to analyze relationships between your people data and key business metrics?**

<--- Score

**92. What employee sentiment data do you currently gather and how do you analyze it?**

<--- Score

93. How sensitive must the MVNO strategy be to cost?

<--- Score

**94. How do you embed people analytics into your organization?**

<--- Score

**95. Does the system provide a measure of progress to the user?**

<--- Score

96. Which measures and indicators matter?

<--- Score

**97. What kind of work is being done in talent analytics?**

<--- Score

**98. How is app/service-specific performance measured and made known to Service Placement Service?**

<--- Score

99. How do you aggregate measures across priorities?

<--- Score

**100. How often should you measure?**

<--- Score

101. Where is it measured?

<--- Score

102. Are missed MVNO opportunities costing your organization money?

<--- Score

103. What are the current costs of the MVNO process?

<--- Score

**104. How do you adopt workforce analytics to address your key business priorities?**

<--- Score

**105. What impact will proactive retention of top performers have on customer value?**

<--- Score

106. What is the total cost related to deploying MVNO, including any consulting or professional services?

<--- Score

107. Have you included everything in your MVNO cost models?

<--- Score

**108. What are your current levels in key measures or indicators of customer satisfaction and dissatisfaction?**

<--- Score

**109. Where do you make an impact?**

<--- Score

110. How can you reduce the costs of obtaining inputs?

<--- Score

**111. What is the vision for a talent analytics function?**

<--- Score

**112. Stakeholder analysis - who do you need to mobilise?**

<--- Score

113. How frequently do you track MVNO measures?

<--- Score

114. What measurements are being captured?

<--- Score

**115. Can you make expert analysts more productive by automating certain repetitive tasks?**

<--- Score

**116. What is your biggest challenge putting people analytics in place and convincing the CEO?**

<--- Score

117. Who is involved in verifying compliance?

<--- Score

118. What causes extra work or rework?
<--- Score

**119. How you measure customer satisfaction?**
<--- Score

**120. How does your organization balance intuition and experience with data and analytics in making decisions?**
<--- Score

**121. Is customer satisfaction measured frequently and regularly?**
<--- Score

122. What relevant entities could be measured?
<--- Score

123. Are actual costs in line with budgeted costs?
<--- Score

**124. How important are hard measurements that show return on investment compared to soft measurements that demonstrate customer satisfaction and public perception?**
<--- Score

**125. How can you reduce Cost and Complexity of Service Provisioning?**
<--- Score

126. How do your measurements capture actionable MVNO information for use in exceeding your customers expectations and securing your customers

engagement?

<--- Score

**127. What technologies and tools do you need to support your analytic capability?**

<--- Score

128. What is measured? Why?

<--- Score

129. What would it cost to replace your technology?

<--- Score

**130. How do you currently measure your customer loyalty?**

<--- Score

Add up total points for this section:
_ _ _ _ _ = Total points for this section

Divided by: _ _ _ _ _ _ (number of statements answered) = _ _ _ _ _ _ Average score for this section

Transfer your score to the MVNO Index at the beginning of the Self-Assessment.

# CRITERION #4: ANALYZE:

INTENT: Analyze causes, assumptions and hypotheses.

In my belief, the answer to this question is clearly defined:

5 Strongly Agree

4 Agree

3 Neutral

2 Disagree

1 Strongly Disagree

**1. How do you qualify the customers?**
<--- Score

2. Is the gap/opportunity displayed and communicated in financial terms?
<--- Score

3. How do you identify specific MVNO investment opportunities and emerging trends?
<--- Score

4. Were Pareto charts (or similar) used to portray the 'heavy hitters' (or key sources of variation)?
<--- Score

**5. Is the Customer Satisfaction Process something which you think can be automated via an IVR?**
<--- Score

6. What are your current levels and trends in key MVNO measures or indicators of product and process performance that are important to and directly serve your customers?
<--- Score

**7. How do you view the MVNO phenomenon in terms of opportunities for MNOs?**
<--- Score

**8. Given your market situation, and your position in it, is FMC an opportunity or a threat?**
<--- Score

**9. Where do you get qualified talent today?**
<--- Score

**10. How are you performing on NPS key drivers relative to competitors?**
<--- Score

11. Were there any improvement opportunities identified from the process analysis?
<--- Score

12. What qualifications are necessary?
<--- Score

**13. Is the customer satisfaction process something which you think can be automated?**
<--- Score

**14. What factors drive employee retention?**
<--- Score

15. What were the crucial 'moments of truth' on the process map?
<--- Score

16. Where is MVNO data gathered?
<--- Score

17. How is MVNO data gathered?
<--- Score

18. What are evaluation criteria for the output?
<--- Score

19. What training and qualifications will you need?
<--- Score

20. Has an output goal been set?
<--- Score

21. What are the personnel training and qualifications required?
<--- Score

22. How is the MVNO Value Stream Mapping managed?
<--- Score

23. Were any designed experiments used to generate

additional insight into the data analysis?
<--- Score

24. What were the financial benefits resulting from any 'ground fruit or low-hanging fruit' (quick fixes)?
<--- Score

25. What are your key performance measures or indicators and in-process measures for the control and improvement of your MVNO processes?
<--- Score

**26. What will be the dealers sale commissioning process?**
<--- Score

**27. Where will m2m and IoT go next and how can MVNOs drive the future?**
<--- Score

**28. What are the opportunities and risks?**
<--- Score

29. Was a detailed process map created to amplify critical steps of the 'as is' stakeholder process?
<--- Score

30. How is the way you as the leader think and process information affecting your organizational culture?
<--- Score

**31. What conditions are imposed during the MVNO licensing process, and what mechanisms are available to mediate commercial relationships between MNOs and MVNOs?**
<--- Score

32. What is your organizations system for selecting qualified vendors?
<--- Score

33. What did the team gain from developing a sub-process map?
<--- Score

34. Do staff qualifications match your project?
<--- Score

35. Are your outputs consistent?
<--- Score

36. Have the problem and goal statements been updated to reflect the additional knowledge gained from the analyze phase?
<--- Score

37. What successful thing are you doing today that may be blinding you to new growth opportunities?
<--- Score

**38. Can the problem of high charges for data roaming services be tackled by wholesale regulation alone?**
<--- Score

39. What conclusions were drawn from the team's data collection and analysis? How did the team reach these conclusions?
<--- Score

40. Do you have the authority to produce the output?
<--- Score

41. Was a cause-and-effect diagram used to explore the different types of causes (or sources of variation)?
<--- Score

42. Is data and process analysis, root cause analysis and quantifying the gap/opportunity in place?
<--- Score

43. Do your contracts/agreements contain data security obligations?
<--- Score

44. How was the detailed process map generated, verified, and validated?
<--- Score

45. Is the MVNO process severely broken such that a re-design is necessary?
<--- Score

46. What qualifications do MVNO leaders need?
<--- Score

**47. How is the data collected?**
<--- Score

**48. When and how will data be disposed of?**
<--- Score

49. Did any additional data need to be collected?
<--- Score

50. What tools were used to narrow the list of possible causes?
<--- Score

51. What quality tools were used to get through the analyze phase?
<--- Score

**52. At what point in the recruitment process do you access information from social media?**
<--- Score

53. What qualifications are needed?
<--- Score

54. Have any additional benefits been identified that will result from closing all or most of the gaps?
<--- Score

55. What are your outputs?
<--- Score

**56. Do mnos view MVNOs as an opportunity or a threat?**
<--- Score

**57. What data do you have and what can you do with it?**
<--- Score

58. How difficult is it to qualify what MVNO ROI is?
<--- Score

59. What process should you select for improvement?
<--- Score

60. How is the data gathered?
<--- Score

61. Who is involved with workflow mapping?
<--- Score

**62. Is there an incremental revenue opportunity?**
<--- Score

**63. Does the system provide the opportunity for cooperation between users?**
<--- Score

64. What do you need to qualify?
<--- Score

**65. Where do the opportunities lie for MVNOs with IoT and M2M?**
<--- Score

66. Did any value-added analysis or 'lean thinking' take place to identify some of the gaps shown on the 'as is' process map?
<--- Score

67. Is pre-qualification of suppliers carried out?
<--- Score

**68. Are you taking adventage of call data?**
<--- Score

**69. Where can MVNOs jump in and seize new opportunities?**
<--- Score

**70. Where do opportunities lie for MVNOs with IoT and M2M?**
<--- Score

71. Is the performance gap determined?
<--- Score

72. What tools were used to generate the list of possible causes?
<--- Score

73. How do mission and objectives affect the MVNO processes of your organization?
<--- Score

74. What are the revised rough estimates of the financial savings/opportunity for MVNO improvements?
<--- Score

**75. How is the data presented?**
<--- Score

76. Are gaps between current performance and the goal performance identified?
<--- Score

77. How do your work systems and key work processes relate to and capitalize on your core competencies?
<--- Score

78. How do you define collaboration and team output?
<--- Score

**79. What are the Opportunities?**
<--- Score

**80. What kind of opportunities does your**

**organization see in the mobile data market?**
<--- Score

81. What does the data say about the performance of the stakeholder process?
<--- Score

82. What are the necessary qualifications?
<--- Score

83. What qualifications and skills do you need?
<--- Score

**84. What are the key business opportunities for value added services in the mobile industry?**
<--- Score

85. What is the cost of poor quality as supported by the team's analysis?
<--- Score

Add up total points for this section:
_ _ _ _ _ = Total points for this section

Divided by: _ _ _ _ _ _ (number of statements answered) = _ _ _ _ _ _
Average score for this section

Transfer your score to the MVNO Index at the beginning of the Self-Assessment.

# CRITERION #5: IMPROVE:

INTENT: Develop a practical solution. Innovate, establish and test the solution and to measure the results.

In my belief, the answer to this question is clearly defined:

5 Strongly Agree

4 Agree

3 Neutral

2 Disagree

1 Strongly Disagree

**1. How does your organization identify and develop talent for critical positions in your organization?**
<--- Score

2. Is the implementation plan designed?
<--- Score

**3. When a MNO decides to conclude a partnership**

**with the MVNO, what is the best wholesale price setting for the partner MNO in order to maximize its profit ?**
<--- Score

4. How will the group know that the solution worked?
<--- Score

5. How do you measure risk?
<--- Score

6. Was a pilot designed for the proposed solution(s)?
<--- Score

**7. What do you do with the results?**
<--- Score

**8. How do you improve customer satisfaction with scorecards?**
<--- Score

9. How do you keep improving MVNO?
<--- Score

**10. How has your network improved compared to its competitors?**
<--- Score

**11. Have public funds contributed to the development of your mobile network?**
<--- Score

12. Is the scope clearly documented?
<--- Score

**13. Do you make sure to ask about your vendor's**

customer satisfaction rating and references in your particular industry. If the vendor does not know its own rating, it may be a red flag that you're dealing with a company that does not put Customer Service at the forefront. How would a company know what to improve if it had no idea what areas customers felt were lacking?
<--- Score

14. Are possible solutions generated and tested?
<--- Score

15. When you map the key players in your own work and the types/domains of relationships with them, which relationships do you find easy and which challenging, and why?
<--- Score

16. Can you identify any significant risks or exposures to MVNO third- parties (vendors, service providers, alliance partners etc) that concern you?
<--- Score

17. Are new and improved process ('should be') maps developed?
<--- Score

**18. How do you improve your transportation logistics to increase customer satisfaction?**
<--- Score

19. Who controls the risk?
<--- Score

20. Are improved process ('should be') maps modified based on pilot data and analysis?

<--- Score

**21. Does your organization expect an improvement in availability or response times that will result in increased user satisfaction?**
<--- Score

22. Risk Identification: What are the possible risk events your organization faces in relation to MVNO?
<--- Score

23. Will the controls trigger any other risks?
<--- Score

**24. The model for improvement - what is it?**
<--- Score

25. Is there a small-scale pilot for proposed improvement(s)? What conclusions were drawn from the outcomes of a pilot?
<--- Score

26. What is the magnitude of the improvements?
<--- Score

**27. As a developer, what metric tools do you need?**
<--- Score

28. For estimation problems, how do you develop an estimation statement?
<--- Score

29. Is there a cost/benefit analysis of optimal solution(s)?
<--- Score

30. Who makes the MVNO decisions in your organization?
<--- Score

**31. What are the Risks?**
<--- Score

32. Are the best solutions selected?
<--- Score

33. What attendant changes will need to be made to ensure that the solution is successful?
<--- Score

**34. In addition to encouraging the next generation of aspiring technology professionals, how does your organization attract and develop technology talent?**
<--- Score

35. What tools do you use once you have decided on a MVNO strategy and more importantly how do you choose?
<--- Score

36. Describe the design of the pilot and what tests were conducted, if any?
<--- Score

**37. To what extent has the emergence of MVNOs overseas resulted in improved outcomes for consumers?**
<--- Score

38. MVNO risk decisions: whose call Is It?
<--- Score

39. What is the team's contingency plan for potential problems occurring in implementation?
<--- Score

**40. What information do participants need to understand partners better?**
<--- Score

41. What actually has to improve and by how much?
<--- Score

42. What resources are required for the improvement efforts?
<--- Score

43. Who are the people involved in developing and implementing MVNO?
<--- Score

**44. What results do you have for key measures or indicators of customer satisfaction and dissatisfaction?**
<--- Score

45. What is the implementation plan?
<--- Score

**46. How does the developer select the breadth of network to be built?**
<--- Score

47. Who will be responsible for making the decisions to include or exclude requested changes once MVNO is underway?
<--- Score

48. What is MVNO's impact on utilizing the best solution(s)?
<--- Score

49. In the past few months, what is the smallest change you have made that has had the biggest positive result? What was it about that small change that produced the large return?
<--- Score

50. What is the risk?
<--- Score

**51. What would you improve?**
<--- Score

**52. What are you hearing businesses asking for as they develop their mobile strategy?**
<--- Score

**53. Do employee empowerment strategies improve unit or organizational performance?**
<--- Score

54. Is pilot data collected and analyzed?
<--- Score

55. What tools were used to tap into the creativity and encourage 'outside the box' thinking?
<--- Score

56. What error proofing will be done to address some of the discrepancies observed in the 'as is' process?
<--- Score

57. What were the underlying assumptions on the cost-benefit analysis?

<--- Score

58. Which of the recognised risks out of all risks can be most likely transferred?

<--- Score

59. How will the team or the process owner(s) monitor the implementation plan to see that it is working as intended?

<--- Score

60. What can you do to improve?

<--- Score

61. What went well, what should change, what can improve?

<--- Score

62. How do you measure progress and evaluate training effectiveness?

<--- Score

63. How did the team generate the list of possible solutions?

<--- Score

64. How does the solution remove the key sources of issues discovered in the analyze phase?

<--- Score

65. How do you improve MVNO service perception, and satisfaction?

<--- Score

66. Is a contingency plan established?
<--- Score

**67. Do you believe that your organization is developing the talent it needs to reach business objectives and meet future challenges?**
<--- Score

**68. What course development tools do you have and what more do you need to purchase?**
<--- Score

69. How do you define the solutions' scope?
<--- Score

**70. What business model is going to be developed?**
<--- Score

71. Are there any constraints (technical, political, cultural, or otherwise) that would inhibit certain solutions?
<--- Score

**72. Do you understand the risk?**
<--- Score

73. Were any criteria developed to assist the team in testing and evaluating potential solutions?
<--- Score

74. Who controls key decisions that will be made?
<--- Score

**75. A clear understanding of the objectives will help to guide companies to the best coworking**

**solution. Is the goal to promote innovation, encourage a cultural change, or attract talent?**
<--- Score

76. Who will be responsible for documenting the MVNO requirements in detail?
<--- Score

77. What does the 'should be' process map/design look like?
<--- Score

78. What needs improvement? Why?
<--- Score

79. Is a solution implementation plan established, including schedule/work breakdown structure, resources, risk management plan, cost/budget, and control plan?
<--- Score

80. What tools were most useful during the improve phase?
<--- Score

81. What improvements have been achieved?
<--- Score

**82. Does the proposed _____ improve your customer relations/satisfaction?**
<--- Score

83. Is supporting MVNO documentation required?
<--- Score

84. What communications are necessary to support

the implementation of the solution?
<--- Score

85. What tools were used to evaluate the potential solutions?
<--- Score

**86. What are the risks for your organization?**
<--- Score

**87. How do you calculate the risk of churning?**
<--- Score

**88. How are customers evaluating current levels of satisfaction across service categories?**
<--- Score

89. What lessons, if any, from a pilot were incorporated into the design of the full-scale solution?
<--- Score

90. How risky is your organization?
<--- Score

91. Do those selected for the MVNO team have a good general understanding of what MVNO is all about?
<--- Score

**92. Will it be used to assemble a talent pool to be developed for future vacancies?**
<--- Score

93. At what point will vulnerability assessments be performed once MVNO is put into production (e.g., ongoing Risk Management after implementation)?
<--- Score

**94. Is there a need to examine the development of a servant leadership style? How do supervisors acquire servant leader characteristics?**
<--- Score

95. Is the optimal solution selected based on testing and analysis?
<--- Score

**96. Can the performance management system develop talent to close the gaps?**
<--- Score

**97. What happens once all eligibility determinations and documentation requirements are complete?**
<--- Score

Add up total points for this section:
_ _ _ _ _ = Total points for this section

Divided by: _ _ _ _ _ _ (number of statements answered) = _ _ _ _ _ _
Average score for this section

Transfer your score to the MVNO Index at the beginning of the Self-Assessment.

# CRITERION #6: CONTROL:

In my belief, the answer to this question is clearly defined:

5 Strongly Agree

4 Agree

3 Neutral

2 Disagree

1 Strongly Disagree

1. What other systems, operations, processes, and infrastructures (hiring practices, staffing, training, incentives/rewards, metrics/dashboards/scorecards, etc.) need updates, additions, changes, or deletions in order to facilitate knowledge transfer and improvements?
<--- Score

2. Does a troubleshooting guide exist or is it needed?

<--- Score

3. Do you monitor the effectiveness of your MVNO activities?
<--- Score

4. Is a response plan in place for when the input, process, or output measures indicate an 'out-of-control' condition?
<--- Score

5. Are suggested corrective/restorative actions indicated on the response plan for known causes to problems that might surface?
<--- Score

6. What are the key elements of your MVNO performance improvement system, including your evaluation, organizational learning, and innovation processes?
<--- Score

7. What should the next improvement project be that is related to MVNO?
<--- Score

8. How will the process owner verify improvement in present and future sigma levels, process capabilities?
<--- Score

9. How widespread is its use?
<--- Score

10. Is knowledge gained on process shared and institutionalized?
<--- Score

**11. Who will benefit from eLearning?**
<--- Score

12. Are documented procedures clear and easy to follow for the operators?
<--- Score

13. Who has control over resources?
<--- Score

**14. When does the MNO plan to roll out 5g under its current business plans?**
<--- Score

15. Is there documentation that will support the successful operation of the improvement?
<--- Score

**16. Can you put your plan on vacation or suspend it?**
<--- Score

17. How likely is the current MVNO plan to come in on schedule or on budget?
<--- Score

18. Is there a documented and implemented monitoring plan?
<--- Score

**19. To what extent can retention be predicted by the variable learning and working climate ?**
<--- Score

**20. What is the learner engagement?**

<--- Score

21. How might the group capture best practices and lessons learned so as to leverage improvements?
<--- Score

22. Has the improved process and its steps been standardized?
<--- Score

23. Are new process steps, standards, and documentation ingrained into normal operations?
<--- Score

**24. What are you planning for?**
<--- Score

25. Is there a recommended audit plan for routine surveillance inspections of MVNO's gains?
<--- Score

26. Do the MVNO decisions you make today help people and the planet tomorrow?
<--- Score

**27. How do you use what you learn about your customers to improve overall customer satisfaction?**
<--- Score

28. Will your goals reflect your program budget?
<--- Score

**29. What advantages can micro-learning provide?**
<--- Score

30. Is reporting being used or needed?
<--- Score

31. Are there documented procedures?
<--- Score

**32. How did you approach the task of developing the right retention management plan for your organization?**
<--- Score

33. Is the MVNO test/monitoring cost justified?
<--- Score

34. Is there a transfer of ownership and knowledge to process owner and process team tasked with the responsibilities.
<--- Score

35. What is the best design framework for MVNO organization now that, in a post industrial-age if the top-down, command and control model is no longer relevant?
<--- Score

36. Does the MVNO performance meet the customer's requirements?
<--- Score

37. Is a response plan established and deployed?
<--- Score

38. Does MVNO appropriately measure and monitor risk?
<--- Score

39. Does job training on the documented procedures need to be part of the process team's education and training?
<--- Score

40. Do you monitor the MVNO decisions made and fine tune them as they evolve?
<--- Score

**41. What are you learning from closed loop processes?**
<--- Score

**42. How does the firm measure and monitor client service and customer satisfaction?**
<--- Score

43. Have new or revised work instructions resulted?
<--- Score

44. How do you select, collect, align, and integrate MVNO data and information for tracking daily operations and overall organizational performance, including progress relative to strategic objectives and action plans?
<--- Score

45. How will new or emerging customer needs/ requirements be checked/communicated to orient the process toward meeting the new specifications and continually reducing variation?
<--- Score

46. Who controls critical resources?
<--- Score

47. What is your theory of human motivation, and how does your compensation plan fit with that view?
<--- Score

48. What do you measure to verify effectiveness gains?
<--- Score

49. Are operating procedures consistent?
<--- Score

**50. Which learning and development priorities does your organization need to focus on Millennials, the true leaders for tomorrow, to realize the talents of younger potential leaders?**
<--- Score

51. What do your reports reflect?
<--- Score

**52. Based upon the business Scenario Plan and Workforce Implications, where does your organization face talent concerns currently or in the future?**
<--- Score

53. Is new knowledge gained imbedded in the response plan?
<--- Score

**54. What will be the geographic reach of the MNOs planned 5G network?**
<--- Score

55. Is there a standardized process?
<--- Score

**56. How do you use learning analytics?**
<--- Score

57. Who is the MVNO process owner?
<--- Score

58. How will report readings be checked to effectively monitor performance?
<--- Score

**59. How does your organization measure and monitor client service and customer satisfaction?**
<--- Score

60. Is there a control plan in place for sustaining improvements (short and long-term)?
<--- Score

61. How will the process owner and team be able to hold the gains?
<--- Score

62. How do you spread information?
<--- Score

63. Are you measuring, monitoring and predicting MVNO activities to optimize operations and profitability, and enhancing outcomes?
<--- Score

64. Will any special training be provided for results interpretation?
<--- Score

65. What is the recommended frequency of auditing?

<--- Score

66. How do you plan for the cost of succession?
<--- Score

**67. How advanced are your plans for 5G networks?**
<--- Score

68. What are your results for key measures or indicators of the accomplishment of your MVNO strategy and action plans, including building and strengthening core competencies?
<--- Score

69. What quality tools were useful in the control phase?
<--- Score

70. How will input, process, and output variables be checked to detect for sub-optimal conditions?
<--- Score

71. What is the control/monitoring plan?
<--- Score

**72. Where do you have talent gaps based on your workforce plan?**
<--- Score

**73. What type of learning do they prefer?**
<--- Score

74. Does the response plan contain a definite closed loop continual improvement scheme (e.g., plan-do-check-act)?
<--- Score

75. How will the day-to-day responsibilities for monitoring and continual improvement be transferred from the improvement team to the process owner?

<--- Score

76. Against what alternative is success being measured?

<--- Score

77. What key inputs and outputs are being measured on an ongoing basis?

<--- Score

78. Are pertinent alerts monitored, analyzed and distributed to appropriate personnel?

<--- Score

**79. What distribution model are you planning to use?**

<--- Score

80. What other areas of the group might benefit from the MVNO team's improvements, knowledge, and learning?

<--- Score

**81. What plans and devices do you have now?**

<--- Score

**82. What should key features of e-learning platforms be kept in mind when researching vendors?**

<--- Score

83. What do you stand for--and what are you against?
<--- Score

**84. Is customer satisfaction information recorded and monitored?**
<--- Score

85. What are the critical parameters to watch?
<--- Score

Add up total points for this section:
_ _ _ _ _  = Total points for this section

Divided by: _ _ _ _ _ _ (number of statements answered) = _ _ _ _ _ _
Average score for this section

Transfer your score to the MVNO Index at the beginning of the Self-Assessment.

# CRITERION #7: SUSTAIN:

INTENT: Retain the benefits.

In my belief, the answer to this question is clearly defined:

5 Strongly Agree

4 Agree

3 Neutral

2 Disagree

1 Strongly Disagree

**1. What kind of talent is in the human cloud?**
<--- Score

2. Is there any existing MVNO governance structure?
<--- Score

**3. Who has checked customer/consumer satisfaction?**
<--- Score

**4. How is the provision of telecoms (or electronic**

**communications) networks and services regulated?**

<--- Score

**5. How to determine pricing to be proposed to MVNO ?**

<--- Score

6. Who else should you help?

<--- Score

7. What have been your experiences in defining long range MVNO goals?

<--- Score

**8. Have you used any social media?**

<--- Score

**9. Customer satisfaction: are your customers satisfied with your products?**

<--- Score

**10. What happens when suppliers downsize?**

<--- Score

**11. To what extent should the MVNO be permitted to set up own infrastructure?**

<--- Score

**12. How are you communicating the benefits of 5G to your customers?**

<--- Score

**13. Do you have the right talent in the right roles to accomplish your mission over the holding period?**

<--- Score

**14. Does the system provide the user with a sense of accomplishment?**
<--- Score

**15. Should there be any roll out obligations specified for MVNO?**
<--- Score

16. Have benefits been optimized with all key stakeholders?
<--- Score

17. How can you incorporate support to ensure safe and effective use of MVNO into the services that you provide?
<--- Score

18. If you were responsible for initiating and implementing major changes in your organization, what steps might you take to ensure acceptance of those changes?
<--- Score

19. How do you engage the workforce, in addition to satisfying them?
<--- Score

**20. Customer-perceived value: a substitute for satisfaction in business markets?**
<--- Score

**21. Can you manage it in other ways?**
<--- Score

**22. Can you maintain turf to customers satisfaction with less water?**
<--- Score

**23. What proportion of your customers do you cover?**
<--- Score

**24. Are you building an effective talent pipeline?**
<--- Score

**25. Is multichannel marketing a segmentation strategy or a customer satisfaction strategy?**
<--- Score

**26. How large is Sprints distribution network compared to AT&T and Verizon?**
<--- Score

27. What happens when a new employee joins the organization?
<--- Score

**28. How deep is your engagement?**
<--- Score

29. What are the barriers to increased MVNO production?
<--- Score

**30. Does it really make things simpler?**
<--- Score

**31. Do loyalty programs increase customers satisfaction with the product/service offering and satisfaction with your organization?**

<--- Score

## 32. For what regions or divisions do you help find talent?
<--- Score

## 33. What is the position of telecom groups towards MVNO ?
<--- Score

## 34. Is your nps good enough?
<--- Score

## 35. How will key account team and executive compensation be tied to service delivery performance and customer satisfaction?
<--- Score

## 36. How does your organization keep track of its human talent?
<--- Score

## 37. Is customer satisfaction an indicator of customer loyalty?
<--- Score

## 38. Is it the right time to introduce MVNO as a distinct service provider with its own licensing and regulatory framework?
<--- Score

## 39. What can be shared and how much can each of the operators save by network sharing?
<--- Score

## 40. MVNOs - do they add value and bring new

services?

<--- Score

**41. What motivates your subscribers to use your network and spend more on your services and products?**

<--- Score

**42. Is your organization doing it right?**

<--- Score

**43. Is the goal to promote innovation, encourage a cultural change, or attract talent?**

<--- Score

**44. What terms or conditions apply to regulated wholesale MVNO access?**

<--- Score

**45. Where next for MVNOs with iot and m2m?**

<--- Score

**46. If core network bandwidth becomes infinite and free , does it matter where services are placed?**

<--- Score

47. Why should you adopt a MVNO framework?

<--- Score

**48. How do MNOs compete to host MVNOs?**

<--- Score

**49. What will be the next generation operational environment?**

<--- Score

**50. How does your organization manage the design and delivery of products and services that promise a high level of customer satisfaction?**
<--- Score

**51. Fixed-mobile convergence: did you miss it?**
<--- Score

**52. Do you have a basic causal sequential relationship between quality, satisfaction and loyalty, and does quality have direct influence on satisfaction and also satisfaction on loyalty?**
<--- Score

**53. Why allow MVNOs to use the MNO network?**
<--- Score

**54. How would you rate the quality of your product?**
<--- Score

**55. How does naas change the channel mix and market positioning?**
<--- Score

**56. What is the conversion path?**
<--- Score

**57. Did your organization experience any acquisitions, sales, mergers, and/or divestitures this year?**
<--- Score

**58. How many units will sell?**
<--- Score

**59. How is service named, described, performance constraints expressed, and registered?**
<--- Score

60. Can you break it down?
<--- Score

61. If you got fired and a new hire took your place, what would she do different?
<--- Score

**62. Who has the best spectrum position and what is it worth?**
<--- Score

**63. Should there be any restriction on cross holdings between two MVNOs and between MVNO and an MNO in a service area?**
<--- Score

**64. Is it a friendly competition with peers?**
<--- Score

**65. How do MNO business models change in the future evolving internet of things?**
<--- Score

**66. Where do you look for talent?**
<--- Score

**67. Does the system include tasks that are meant to be solved in a group?**
<--- Score

**68. What is your current level of customer satisfaction?**

<--- Score

**69. How have the competitive conditions changed in the wholesale mobile services market?**
<--- Score

70. What is the overall business strategy?
<--- Score

**71. What is the level of performance in terms of productivity, customer satisfaction, quality, etc?**
<--- Score

**72. How often do you ask customers?**
<--- Score

**73. Will you offer product bundling?**
<--- Score

**74. Do you see any imminent threat?**
<--- Score

**75. Will you use SMS aggregators?**
<--- Score

**76. Do you have an effective governance structure?**
<--- Score

**77. How do you use conversions?**
<--- Score

**78. What kind of systems conduct the logging?**
<--- Score

**79. Where will the services come from?**

<--- Score

## 80. What is a good score?
<--- Score

81. How do you deal with MVNO changes?
<--- Score

## 82. Why should top talent work for you?
<--- Score

## 83. Predicting attrition is interesting, and then, what do you do with it?
<--- Score

## 84. Which is the more desirable criterion and by how much, customer satisfaction or business value?
<--- Score

## 85. Is the I-mode business model becoming extinct?
<--- Score

86. Did your employees make progress today?
<--- Score

## 87. Do you believe that wholesale SMS roaming charges (IOTs) should be regulated?
<--- Score

88. How will you ensure you get what you expected?
<--- Score

## 89. How will your organization leverage its resources to Hire and Retain a talented workforce?

<--- Score

**90. Has customer satisfaction in each channel increased, remained flat, or decreased?**
<--- Score

91. Were lessons learned captured and communicated?
<--- Score

92. What are the success criteria that will indicate that MVNO objectives have been met and the benefits delivered?
<--- Score

93. Are new benefits received and understood?
<--- Score

94. Can you do all this work?
<--- Score

**95. How is customer satisfaction maintained?**
<--- Score

96. What are you trying to prove to yourself, and how might it be hijacking your life and business success?
<--- Score

**97. How will you charge for roaming services?**
<--- Score

**98. How will you operate changes to the HLR profiles?**
<--- Score

99. If you find that you havent accomplished one of

the goals for one of the steps of the MVNO strategy, what will you do to fix it?

<--- Score

**100. How many customers do you expect to serve?**

<--- Score

**101. What keeps your cfo, cio, it managers and network operators up at night?**

<--- Score

**102. What kind of time frame do you foresee?**

<--- Score

**103. What should be the method and consideration for determining the entry fee for MVNO?**

<--- Score

**104. What are your organizations activities that affect customer satisfaction?**

<--- Score

**105. Should there be any restriction on the number of MVNOs attached to an MNO?**

<--- Score

**106. How niche can you get as an MVNO?**

<--- Score

**107. How would you characterize your organizations customer satisfaction?**

<--- Score

**108. What information should be easily accessible?**

<--- Score

**109. How will your organization create value?**

<--- Score

**110. Is wholesale roaming regulated?**

<--- Score

111. Has implementation been effective in reaching specified objectives so far?

<--- Score

**112. What share of the termination fee (created by customers) do MVNOs get?**

<--- Score

**113. What tools do you use to do inbound sales?**

<--- Score

114. Is MVNO dependent on the successful delivery of a current project?

<--- Score

**115. In terms of customer service satisfaction, is there any study done after the implementation?**

<--- Score

116. What are the rules and assumptions your industry operates under? What if the opposite were true?

<--- Score

**117. Do customer relationship management applications affect customer satisfaction?**

<--- Score

**118. What makes a great KPI?**

<--- Score

**119. If core network bandwidth becomes infinite and free, does it matter where services are placed?**
<--- Score

**120. What would make the 5G service business more attractive to your organization?**
<--- Score

121. Is the MVNO organization completing tasks effectively and efficiently?
<--- Score

**122. What are the roles of customer satisfaction and perceived value in producing online customer loyalty?**
<--- Score

**123. Why will my organization deliver customer satisfaction?**
<--- Score

**124. Do you have a referral marketing program?**
<--- Score

**125. Relevant -are you measuring/benchmarking what is easy even if it is not really relevant to the company or customer satisfaction?**
<--- Score

**126. What work-related activities within your organization promote employee retention?**
<--- Score

127. When information truly is ubiquitous, when reach and connectivity are completely global, when

computing resources are infinite, and when a whole new set of impossibilities are not only possible, but happening, what will that do to your business?
<--- Score

**128. How have business consumers perceptions towards your organization changed since last year?**
<--- Score

**129. How do the business objectives of the participants mesh with each other?**
<--- Score

**130. Do you observe marked difference between full and light MVNOs?**
<--- Score

**131. What do clients truly value?**
<--- Score

132. What are the usability implications of MVNO actions?
<--- Score

**133. Can universities serve as a source of category management talent?**
<--- Score

**134. Are you losing critical talent?**
<--- Score

**135. Do you feel that you are currently in the position that best suits your skills and talents?**
<--- Score

**136. How is customer satisfaction gauged?**

<--- Score

**137. What is the turnover rate for diverse talent?**

<--- Score

**138. What would you expect as a customer?**

<--- Score

**139. Can operators see each others settings?**

<--- Score

**140. Are ratings for customer satisfaction and product quality displayed?**

<--- Score

**141. When will you deliver customer satisfaction?**

<--- Score

142. Do you have past MVNO successes?

<--- Score

**143. Do you have a way to actively meter and manage your network usage?**

<--- Score

**144. To what extent are MVNOs creating competitive pressures in the mobile telecommunications sector?**

<--- Score

145. Are you paying enough attention to the partners your company depends on to succeed?

<--- Score

**146. What is the method and consideration for**

**determining the entry fee for MVNO?**
<--- Score

147. What is the craziest thing you can do?
<--- Score

**148. Does the system provide tangible rewards to the user?**
<--- Score

**149. What type of NPS growth does your organization attempt to achieve?**
<--- Score

**150. What is your customer loyalty?**
<--- Score

**151. What are the most important features of a mobile service for your business consumers?**
<--- Score

**152. What should be the eligibility criteria for MVNO?**
<--- Score

**153. How are quality and customer satisfaction related?**
<--- Score

**154. What are the Service revenues / network capex+opex ?**
<--- Score

155. How much contingency will be available in the budget?
<--- Score

**156. Are roaming rates for smaller networks / new entrants regulated?**
<--- Score

**157. How many questions do you ask?**
<--- Score

**158. In competition law, what is an abuse of a dominant position?**
<--- Score

**159. Do you ask: Based on your most recent experience, how likely is it that you would recommend your brand to a friend or colleague?**
<--- Score

**160. Are wearables and the IoT, and other embedded applications the next major phase?**
<--- Score

**161. How fast are you growing your talent pool?**
<--- Score

162. Marketing budgets are tighter, consumers are more skeptical, and social media has changed forever the way we talk about MVNO. How do you gain traction?
<--- Score

**163. How do you determine customer satisfaction, engagement, and dissatisfacction?**
<--- Score

**164. What kind of resources and assets does a full MVNO have?**

<--- Score

**165. Do you currently know your referral quotient?**
<--- Score

**166. Is it the same training material for every team member?**
<--- Score

**167. In the open mobile era, how can you as a mobile operator defend your position in the value network?**
<--- Score

**168. What happens if you buy a device that does not fully support your carriers network?**
<--- Score

169. Do you have enough freaky customers in your portfolio pushing you to the limit day in and day out?
<--- Score

170. Do you think MVNO accomplishes the goals you expect it to accomplish?
<--- Score

**171. Are the participants sharing a common business goal, or simply links in a supply chain?**
<--- Score

172. Are there any activities that you can take off your to do list?
<--- Score

**173. Are you going to allow for some of your customers negative balances?**

<--- Score

174. Is the impact that MVNO has shown?
<--- Score

**175. Do you know where your talent is?**
<--- Score

176. Who are four people whose careers you have enhanced?
<--- Score

177. What do we do when new problems arise?
<--- Score

178. Instead of going to current contacts for new ideas, what if you reconnected with dormant contacts--the people you used to know?  If you were going reactivate a dormant tie, who would it be?
<--- Score

179. What have you done to protect your business from competitive encroachment?
<--- Score

**180. Where do you use NPS to enhance your customer service and customer satisfaction?**
<--- Score

**181. Should regulators set rates to terminate calls on mobile networks?**
<--- Score

182. Who do we want your customers to become?
<--- Score

**183. Will you have one-time charges/fees?**
<--- Score

184. Do you know who is a friend or a foe?
<--- Score

**185. Will you have any content provider or other Value Added Services partners?**
<--- Score

**186. Are there wholesale substitutes for SMS termination?**
<--- Score

187. Will there be any necessary staff changes (redundancies or new hires)?
<--- Score

**188. Will MNOs leverage edge computing to gain competitive advantage over the OTTS?**
<--- Score

**189. What log format is being used?**
<--- Score

**190. What technologies for project work do you promote?**
<--- Score

**191. What kind of customers will you support (prepaid, postpaid, hybrid)?**
<--- Score

**192. What is a good NPS score?**
<--- Score

193. What are specific MVNO rules to follow?
<--- Score

**194. What is your level of exposure?**
<--- Score

**195. Where are you today?**
<--- Score

**196. Did you know?**
<--- Score

197. How do you accomplish your long range MVNO goals?
<--- Score

198. Operational - will it work?
<--- Score

199. Why is it important to have senior management support for a MVNO project?
<--- Score

**200. What can the MVNO offer enterprise customers, that the MNO can not?**
<--- Score

201. What is effective MVNO?
<--- Score

**202. How does your preferred business model contribute to each objectives?**
<--- Score

**203. Where do you find fault with NPS?**
<--- Score

**204. What techniques are applied to implement traffic steering in practice?**

<--- Score

205. Who is the main stakeholder, with ultimate responsibility for driving MVNO forward?

<--- Score

**206. How do mobile operators position themselves in the value chain?**

<--- Score

**207. What business is your customer in?**

<--- Score

**208. Which terms do you have?**

<--- Score

**209. How do you help customers grow?**

<--- Score

**210. Safety benefits: what is the customer satisfaction (or lack thereof) with the system?**

<--- Score

211. How do you keep records, of what?

<--- Score

**212. How valuable is word of mouth?**

<--- Score

**213. Are MVNOs able to negotiate competitive wholesale access arrangements with mnos?**

<--- Score

214. How do you foster the skills, knowledge, talents, attributes, and characteristics you want to have?
<--- Score

215. If you had to rebuild your organization without any traditional competitive advantages (i.e., no killer a technology, promising research, innovative product/ service delivery model, etc.), how would your people have to approach their work and collaborate together in order to create the necessary conditions for success?
<--- Score

216. When should you bother with diagrams?
<--- Score

**217. How can social networking communities be brought to the mobile environment?**
<--- Score

**218. What has happened recently?**
<--- Score

**219. How do you keep track of where everything is?**
<--- Score

**220. How are you going to grow the culture?**
<--- Score

**221. What reports will be relevant to you to follow-up on the business and operational efficiency?**
<--- Score

222. How do you stay inspired?
<--- Score

**223. What is the customer satisfaction rate?**
<--- Score

**224. Does your organization practice retention efforts?**
<--- Score

**225. Can you cross-sell with other existing businesses?**
<--- Score

226. Who is responsible for ensuring appropriate resources (time, people and money) are allocated to MVNO?
<--- Score

**227. Do you share customer satisfaction ratings with customers?**
<--- Score

**228. What is the Market share per product / business?**
<--- Score

**229. How is the sharing of spectrum done between the MNO and MVNO?**
<--- Score

**230. Who participates?**
<--- Score

231. How do you provide a safe environment -physically and emotionally?
<--- Score

**232. On what basis are MVNO services provided and is this consistent with other MVNOs?**
<--- Score

**233. Whose towers are being used and what is the coverage?**
<--- Score

**234. How does quality of place shape attraction and retention in your organization?**
<--- Score

235. What is the source of the strategies for MVNO strengthening and reform?
<--- Score

**236. Are you at the same place your larger peers are?**
<--- Score

**237. How are wholesale agreements for SMS termination currently structured?**
<--- Score

**238. What do you see as a major challenge for talent acquisition and retention?**
<--- Score

239. What trophy do you want on your mantle?
<--- Score

**240. The talent is out there - how do you find it?**
<--- Score

**241. Are customers disadvantaged by bundling mobile services?**

&lt;--- Score

## 242. What is a barrier to entry?
&lt;--- Score

## 243. Who will be your partners for SIM card manufacturing?
&lt;--- Score

244. If there were zero limitations, what would you do differently?
&lt;--- Score

245. How long will it take to change?
&lt;--- Score

## 246. Will this be enough to make your customers churn, or is it too little, too late?
&lt;--- Score

247. How do you govern and fulfill your societal responsibilities?
&lt;--- Score

## 248. Do you have the right numbers of talented people?
&lt;--- Score

## 249. Do you have existing contracts to contend with?
&lt;--- Score

## 250. What are the phases of your inbound sales strategy?
&lt;--- Score

**251. What is the share of post-paid contracts?**
<--- Score

**252. What contributes most to satisfaction and retention?**
<--- Score

**253. Using customer satisfaction as an index of organizational performance, does customer satisfaction increase over time as managers are selected?**
<--- Score

**254. Is your network prepared?**
<--- Score

**255. The technology poses fundamental questions for the role of mobile operators. If devices can communicate directly, where does it leave the carriers?**
<--- Score

**256. Is customer satisfaction mediating the effect of customer-perceived value on customer loyalty?**
<--- Score

**257. What are the critical components of the service?**
<--- Score

**258. What are the challenges of using LTE for public safety networks?**
<--- Score

259. How does MVNO integrate with other stakeholder initiatives?

<--- Score

**260. How does sprints network footprint compare nationally to that of verizon and at&t?**
<--- Score

**261. If each internal vendor understood that their tenure with the organization hinged totally on the satisfaction of their internal customers, might their behavior be different?**
<--- Score

**262. Has your organization been able to recruit and retain talent competitively?**
<--- Score

**263. Does the system give the user a feeling of competence?**
<--- Score

**264. How do you perform customer satisfaction surveys?**
<--- Score

265. What projects are going on in the organization today, and what resources are those projects using from the resource pools?
<--- Score

266. If no one would ever find out about your accomplishments, how would you lead differently?
<--- Score

267. Do you know what you are doing? And who do you call if you don't?
<--- Score

**268. Has customer satisfaction with your service been assessed?**

<--- Score

**269. Why will my organization deliver this particular customer satisfaction?**

<--- Score

270. What should you stop doing?

<--- Score

**271. What concrete protections can you commit to for your prepaid customers?**

<--- Score

**272. What is driving growth?**

<--- Score

**273. Where is the actual bottleneck in mobile networks?**

<--- Score

274. What counts that you are not counting?

<--- Score

**275. How will you attract more customers and retain existing ones?**

<--- Score

**276. What do you see as the biggest employee retention challenge in the future?**

<--- Score

**277. How do you attract customers?**

<--- Score

**278. How do you determine customer satisfaction, and engagement?**

<--- Score

**279. How are MVNOs positioning themselves alongside convergent services?**

<--- Score

280. Is it economical; do you have the time and money?

<--- Score

**281. How often do you ask customers the NPS question?**

<--- Score

**282. Where are the skills and talent gaps in your workforce?**

<--- Score

**283. How are you driving and measuring customer satisfaction?**

<--- Score

284. Have new benefits been realized?

<--- Score

285. What could happen if you do not do it?

<--- Score

**286. Are there wholesale substitutes for mobile voice call termination?**

<--- Score

**287. Do you think that holacracy is a good match**

**with your business strategy?**
<--- Score

**288. What are you seeing as far as market dynamics and the availability of talent?**
<--- Score

**289. Do you ask: Have I handled this call to your satisfaction?**
<--- Score

**290. Should you use SCORM?**
<--- Score

291. Who will manage the integration of tools?
<--- Score

**292. Any way to build a network?**
<--- Score

**293. Should MVNO access to MNO networks be regulated?**
<--- Score

294. Why will customers want to buy your organizations products/services?
<--- Score

**295. Can your organization communicate?**
<--- Score

**296. What do your customers wish you had that you do not have?**
<--- Score

**297. How do you register as a mobile consumer?**

<--- Score

## 298. Do you have high approval/ customer satisfaction ratings?
<--- Score

## 299. Who will be your partners for scratch card manufacturing?
<--- Score

300. What is the purpose of MVNO in relation to the mission?
<--- Score

## 301. Will more regional and rural customers have a choice of provider?
<--- Score

## 302. Do you have any roaming partners or will you only use your MNOs agreements?
<--- Score

## 303. Do you know, whether your MNO offers different contract structures for different MVNOs/ MSOs?
<--- Score

## 304. Is mobile wimax a viable alternative to an MVNO agreement with a 3g network provider?
<--- Score

## 305. Why is it that in most of the markets there are a few MVNOs with a majority customer share and a long tail of struggling MVNOs?
<--- Score

**306. How can MVNOs be sure they have easy access to network intelligence?**
<--- Score

**307. What tools are used for customer success?**
<--- Score

**308. What is the effect of a recommendation?**
<--- Score

**309. Do you have the right quality of talent?**
<--- Score

**310. What do you see as being the most critical business challenges that real-time charging can address?**
<--- Score

**311. Will you have any interconnect partners or will you use your MNOs agreements?**
<--- Score

312. Is your strategy driving your strategy? Or is the way in which you allocate resources driving your strategy?
<--- Score

**313. What percentage of SMS traffic is carried by each technology used to deliver it?**
<--- Score

314. Are your responses positive or negative?
<--- Score

**315. How will carriers handle the evolution of 5g?**
<--- Score

### 316. What should be the eligibility criteria for new MVNOs?

<--- Score

### 317. How will you deliver customer satisfaction?

<--- Score

### 318. What are you going to see in 10 years time?

<--- Score

### 319. How do you compare?

<--- Score

### 320. Job Satisfaction and Job performance: Is the relationship spurious?

<--- Score

321. Whose voice (department, ethnic group, women, older workers, etc) might you have missed hearing from in your company, and how might you amplify this voice to create positive momentum for your business?

<--- Score

### 322. How are you performing in different customer segments?

<--- Score

### 323. How will your organization position itself in the marketplace?

<--- Score

### 324. What are the factors that are driving retention rate in your organization?

<--- Score

**325. For whom will your organization create value?**
<--- Score

326. Do you feel that more should be done in the MVNO area?
<--- Score

327. Who are the key stakeholders?
<--- Score

**328. What is your inbound marketing?**
<--- Score

**329. Why would MNOs go along?**
<--- Score

**330. How can operators and OEMs join the project?**
<--- Score

**331. Is your nps survey automated?**
<--- Score

**332. Does the design support and empower workers and allow their talents to be used to best advantage?**
<--- Score

**333. What should be the service obligations of MVNO?**
<--- Score

**334. What should executives do to deliver on the promise of employee engagement?**

<--- Score

335. Is maximizing MVNO protection the same as minimizing MVNO loss?
<--- Score

336. What will be the consequences to the stakeholder (financial, reputation etc) if MVNO does not go ahead or fails to deliver the objectives?
<--- Score

**337. What strategies, if any, does your organization currently have in place to encourage employee retention?**
<--- Score

**338. How is network-to-network interconnection and access mandated?**
<--- Score

**339. How does sprints network performance compare to that of verizon and at&t?**
<--- Score

**340. Number portability for vno - whether or not, how?**
<--- Score

**341. Does the current or future labor market indicate the appropriate availability of talent for which your organization is competitive?**
<--- Score

**342. What is the economic premise for the existence of a voluntary MNO-MVNO relationship?**
<--- Score

**343. Who will deliver customer satisfaction?**
<--- Score

344. Do you have the right capabilities and capacities?
<--- Score

**345. What empowers your firm to effectively command employees?**
<--- Score

**346. How is your network coverage and user penetration today?**
<--- Score

347. What is the overall talent health of your organization as a whole at senior levels, and for each organization reporting to a member of the Senior Leadership Team?
<--- Score

**348. Do you think MVNO should be subjected to Universal Access obligations?**
<--- Score

**349. What are the phases of mobile forensics?**
<--- Score

**350. Should wholesale regulation be maintained and, if so, for how long?**
<--- Score

**351. How does your organization add value and increase customers willingness to pay for their products?**
<--- Score

**352. How does your organization compete for enterprise and government customers?**
<--- Score

**353. How do you conduct a customer satisfaction survey?**
<--- Score

**354. What is the effect of WiMAX cannibalization on existing 3G networks?**
<--- Score

**355. Customer satisfaction : How happy are they?**
<--- Score

**356. What resources, talents and experiences will you draw upon to complete the work of the proposed program?**
<--- Score

**357. What is the conversion rate?**
<--- Score

**358. How does your organization promote employee retention?**
<--- Score

**359. Where will you deliver customer satisfaction?**
<--- Score

**360. Do managers selected using the predictors to customer satisfaction tend to have more satisfied customers (i.e., higher team-based customer satisfaction scores) than the comparison group?**
<--- Score

**361. Are there some cultures where servant leadership is less effective?**

<--- Score

**362. How likely is it that you would recommend your organization / product / service to a friend or colleague?**

<--- Score

**363. Do multi-product customers tend to be higher margin customers?**

<--- Score

364. What are the challenges?

<--- Score

**365. What is the shape of evolving technologies?**

<--- Score

366. How do you manage MVNO Knowledge Management (KM)?

<--- Score

**367. What channels will you use for self care?**

<--- Score

**368. What will the free cash flow be next year?**

<--- Score

**369. What is the right MVNO business model?**

<--- Score

**370. Why do customer relationship management applications affect customer satisfaction?**

<--- Score

### 371. How do customer relationship management applications affect customer satisfaction?

<--- Score

### 372. Are you a talent magnet?

<--- Score

### 373. How would you rate your organization?

<--- Score

### 374. Can MVNOs reduce dependency on network hosts with mobile wimax?

<--- Score

375. How do you lead with MVNO in mind?
<--- Score

376. Do you say no to customers for no reason?
<--- Score

### 377. Can social networks substitute SMS usage?

<--- Score

### 378. What factors are important?

<--- Score

379. What is the estimated value of the project?
<--- Score

### 380. Is it only full MVNOs who have sufficient access to the network?

<--- Score

### 381. What are the operation strategies for your MVNO business?

<--- Score

**382. Throughput rates: how do they relate?**
<--- Score

**383. Which is necessary for the success of employee empowerment?**
<--- Score

**384. Who will be the Network-as-a-Service provider of the future?**
<--- Score

385. What are current MVNO paradigms?
<--- Score

**386. How you are positioning your organization?**
<--- Score

**387. What should be the FDI limit for MVNO?**
<--- Score

**388. Is multichannel customer management a segmentation strategy or a customer satisfaction strategy?**
<--- Score

**389. What is your IoT strategy?**
<--- Score

**390. What is your organizations lead nurturing?**
<--- Score

**391. Does it matter if china beats the US to build a 5g network?**
<--- Score

**392. Whats the best way to conduct a customer satisfaction survey?**

<--- Score

**393. How do you as a MVNO deliver and exceed on promises to your customers?**

<--- Score

**394. How do the mnos compete to host MVNOs?**

<--- Score

**395. What is the MVNO looking for in an MVNO partnership?**

<--- Score

396. What should a proof of concept or pilot accomplish?

<--- Score

**397. Is the relationship a business-to-business or supplier-to-buyer one?**

<--- Score

398. If your customer were your grandmother, would you tell her to buy what you're selling?

<--- Score

**399. What information do you want from your customers, what is valuable to you?**

<--- Score

**400. Why is a vibrant mobile wholesale market important for businesses and consumers?**

<--- Score

**401. How strongly do you agree that organization X makes it easy for you to do business with it?**
<--- Score

**402. The network : are you behind it or ahead of it?**
<--- Score

**403. With the emergence of MNO sub-brands, what happens to MVNOs in a market?**
<--- Score

Add up total points for this section:
_____ = Total points for this section

Divided by: _____ (number of statements answered) = _____
Average score for this section

Transfer your score to the MVNO Index at the beginning of the Self-Assessment.

# MVNO and Managing Projects, Criteria for Project Managers:

# 1.0 Initiating Process Group: MVNO

1. What were things that you did well, and could improve, and how?

2. Where must it be done?

3. Specific - is the objective clear in terms of what, how, when, and where the situation will be changed?

4. Do you know the roles & responsibilities required for this MVNO project?

5. Contingency planning. if a risk event occurs, what will you do?

6. What input will you be required to provide the MVNO project team?

7. Who is funding the MVNO project?

8. What are the required resources?

9. Although the MVNO project manager does not directly manage procurement and contracting activities, who does manage procurement and contracting activities in your organization then if not the PM?

10. Are stakeholders properly informed about the status of the MVNO project?

11. Have the stakeholders identified all individual requirements pertaining to business process?

12. Who is involved in each phase?

13. Measurable - are the targets measurable?

14. Were escalated issues resolved promptly?

15. When are the deliverables to be generated in each phase?

16. How will you know you did it?

17. Which six sigma dmaic phase focuses on why and how defects and errors occur?

18. Did you use a contractor or vendor?

19. How will you do it?

20. Who does what?

# 1.1 Project Charter: MVNO

21. What barriers do you predict to your success?

22. How high should you set your goals?

23. What metrics could you look at?

24. How will you learn more about the process or system you are trying to improve?

25. Did your MVNO project ask for this?

26. Assumptions and constraints: what assumptions were made in defining the MVNO project?

27. What are the deliverables?

28. What are the known stakeholder requirements?

29. Why do you need to manage scope?

30. Why Outsource?

31. How will you know a change is an improvement?

32. Where does all this information come from?

33. Major high-level milestone targets: what events measure progress?

34. What date will the task finish?

35. What is the purpose of the MVNO project?

36. What changes can you make to improve?

37. When will this occur?

38. Fit with other Products Compliments – Cannibalizes?

39. What are the assigned resources?

40. Avoid costs, improve service, and/ or comply with a mandate?

# 1.2 Stakeholder Register: MVNO

41. How will reports be created?

42. What are the major MVNO project milestones requiring communications or providing communications opportunities?

43. What opportunities exist to provide communications?

44. How big is the gap?

45. Who are the stakeholders?

46. How much influence do they have on the MVNO project?

47. What & Why?

48. Is your organization ready for change?

49. How should employers make voices heard?

50. What is the power of the stakeholder?

51. Who is managing stakeholder engagement?

52. Who wants to talk about Security?

# 1.3 Stakeholder Analysis Matrix: MVNO

53. What obstacles does your organization face?

54. Where are the good opportunities facing your organizations development?

55. Accreditations, etc?

56. What is relationship with the MVNO project?

57. It developments?

58. Does the stakeholder want to be involved or merely need to be informed about the MVNO project and its process?

59. How can you counter negative efforts?

60. Continuity, supply chain robustness?

61. What mechanisms are proposed to monitor and measure MVNO project performance in terms of social development outcomes?

62. Philosophy and values?

63. Cashflow, start-up cash-drain?

64. How will the stakeholder directly benefit from the MVNO project and how will this affect the stakeholders motivation?

65. Are you working on the right risks?

66. Which conditions out of the control of the management are crucial for the sustainability of its effects?

67. Processes and systems, etc?

68. What is the stakeholders power and status in relation to the MVNO project?

69. How to involve media?

70. Will the impacts be local, national or international?

71. Beneficiaries; who are the potential beneficiaries?

72. Are there people who ise voices or interests in the issue may not be heard?

# 2.0 Planning Process Group: MVNO

73. How are the principles of aid effectiveness (ownership, alignment, management for development results and mutual responsibility) being applied in the MVNO project?

74. How well will the chosen processes produce the expected results?

75. Do the partners have sufficient financial capacity to keep up the benefits produced by the programme?

76. If a task is partitionable, is this a sufficient condition to reduce the MVNO project duration?

77. Are the follow-up indicators relevant and do they meet the quality needed to measure the outputs and outcomes of the MVNO project?

78. How many days can task X be late in starting without affecting the MVNO project completion date?

79. How are it MVNO projects different?

80. What are the different approaches to building the WBS?

81. What good practices or successful experiences or transferable examples have been identified?

82. How should needs be met?

83. On which process should team members spend

the most time?

84. Is the duration of the program sufficient to ensure a cycle that will MVNO project the sustainability of the interventions?

85. What factors are contributing to progress or delay in the achievement of products and results?

86. How can you make your needs known?

87. If action is called for, what form should it take?

88. Just how important is your work to the overall success of the MVNO project?

89. Will you be replaced?

90. To what extent do the intervention objectives and strategies of the MVNO project respond to your organizations plans?

# 2.1 Project Management Plan: MVNO

91. Development trends and opportunities. What if the positive direction and vision of your organization causes expected trends to change?

92. What are the assumptions?

93. Do there need to be organizational changes?

94. Are the proposed MVNO project purposes different than a previously authorized MVNO project?

95. Are the existing and future without-plan conditions reasonable and appropriate?

96. What worked well?

97. Is the budget realistic?

98. What happened during the process that you found interesting?

99. How do you manage integration?

100. How do you manage time?

101. Why do you manage integration?

102. What are the constraints?

103. What data/reports/tools/etc. do your PMs need?

104. What is the business need?

105. Are alternatives safe, functional, constructible, economical, reasonable and sustainable?

106. Are there any windfall benefits that would accrue to the MVNO project sponsor or other parties?

107. How well are you able to manage your risk?

108. Is the engineering content at a feasibility level-of-detail, and is it sufficiently complete, to provide an adequate basis for the baseline cost estimate?

109. How do you organize the costs in the MVNO project management plan?

# 2.2 Scope Management Plan: MVNO

110. Is the MVNO project sponsor clearly communicating the business case or rationale for why this MVNO project is needed?

111. Is a pmo (MVNO project management office) in place and provide oversight to the MVNO project?

112. Materials available for performing the work?

113. Does the resource management plan include a personnel development plan?

114. Is the schedule updated on a periodic basis?

115. Are the payment terms being followed?

116. Are software metrics formally captured, analyzed and used as a basis for other MVNO project estimates?

117. Are enough systems & user personnel assigned to the MVNO project?

118. Does the business case include how the MVNO project aligns with your organizations strategic goals & objectives?

119. Is stakeholder involvement adequate?

120. Where do scope management processes fit in?

121. Have adequate procedures been put in place for MVNO project communication and status reporting

across MVNO project boundaries (for example interdependent software development among interfacing systems)?

122. How much money have you spent?

123. Is the MVNO project status reviewed with the steering and executive teams at appropriate intervals?

124. What is your organizations history in doing similar activities?

125. Will the MVNO project deliverables become accepted in writing?

126. Are risk oriented checklists used during risk identification?

127. Is there a Steering Committee in place?

128. Do you have funding for MVNO project and product development, implementation and on-going support?

129. To whom will the deliverables be first presented for inspection and verification?

## 2.3 Requirements Management Plan: MVNO

130. Who came up with this requirement?

131. How often will the reporting occur?

132. Who is responsible for monitoring and tracking the MVNO project requirements?

133. To see if a requirement statement is sufficiently well-defined, read it from the developers perspective. Mentally add the phrase, call me when youre done to the end of the requirement and see if that makes you nervous. In other words, would you need additional clarification from the author to understand the requirement well enough to design and implement it?

134. How detailed should the MVNO project get?

135. Will you use an assessment of the MVNO project environment as a tool to discover risk to the requirements process?

136. Who will initially review the MVNO project work or products to ensure it meets the applicable acceptance criteria?

137. Did you provide clear and concise specifications?

138. Could inaccurate or incomplete requirements in this MVNO project create a serious risk for the business?

139. How will you communicate scheduled tasks to other team members?

140. Is the system software (non-operating system) new to the IT MVNO project team?

141. What cost metrics will be used?

142. How will bidders price evaluations be done, by deliverables, phases, or in a big bang?

143. Why manage requirements?

144. What is the earliest finish date for this MVNO project if it is scheduled to start on ...?

145. Business analysis scope?

146. Does the MVNO project have a Change Control process?

147. Subject to change control?

148. When and how will a requirements baseline be established in this MVNO project?

149. Do you have an agreed upon process for alerting the MVNO project Manager if a request for change in requirements leads to a product scope change?

## 2.4 Requirements Documentation: MVNO

150. Where do system and software requirements come from, what are sources?

151. Is the requirement properly understood?

152. What is the risk associated with the technology?

153. What happens when requirements are wrong?

154. Does the system provide the functions which best support the customers needs?

155. How to document system requirements?

156. Is the origin of the requirement clearly stated?

157. Has requirements gathering uncovered information that would necessitate changes?

158. What are the attributes of a customer?

159. How does the proposed MVNO project contribute to the overall objectives of your organization?

160. Where do you define what is a customer, what are the attributes of customer?

161. Does your organization restrict technical alternatives?

162. What is a show stopper in the requirements?

163. Is the requirement realistically testable?

164. Do technical resources exist?

165. How do you get the user to tell you what they want?

166. Verifiability. can the requirements be checked?

167. How does what is being described meet the business need?

168. What is your Elevator Speech?

169. Who is interacting with the system?

# 2.5 Requirements Traceability Matrix: MVNO

170. What are the chronologies, contingencies, consequences, criteria?

171. Will you use a Requirements Traceability Matrix?

172. How do you manage scope?

173. Describe the process for approving requirements so they can be added to the traceability matrix and MVNO project work can be performed. Will the MVNO project requirements become approved in writing?

174. What percentage of MVNO projects are producing traceability matrices between requirements and other work products?

175. Do you have a clear understanding of all subcontracts in place?

176. How will it affect the stakeholders personally in their career?

177. Why use a WBS?

178. Why do you manage scope?

179. Is there a requirements traceability process in place?

180. What is the WBS?

## 181. How small is small enough?

# 2.6 Project Scope Statement: MVNO

182. Is there a baseline plan against which to measure progress?

183. Is this process communicated to the customer and team members?

184. Is an issue management process documented and filed?

185. Have you been able to thoroughly document the MVNO projects assumptions and constraints?

186. Will statistics related to QA be collected, trends analyzed, and problems raised as issues?

187. Write a brief purpose statement for this MVNO project. Include a business justification statement. What is the product of this MVNO project?

188. Has the MVNO project scope statement been reviewed as part of the baseline process?

189. Relevant - ask yourself can you get there; why are you doing this MVNO project?

190. How often do you estimate that the scope might change, and why?

191. What are the major deliverables of the MVNO project?

192. Have you been able to easily identify success

criteria and create objective measurements for each of the MVNO project scopes goal statements?

193. Is the quality function identified and assigned?

194. Is there an information system for the MVNO project?

195. Was planning completed before the MVNO project was initiated?

196. Any new risks introduced or old risks impacted. Are there issues that could affect the existing requirements for the result, service, or product if the scope changes?

197. Do you anticipate new stakeholders joining the MVNO project over time?

198. Is the MVNO project manager qualified and experienced in MVNO project management?

199. What went right?

200. If the scope changes, what will the impact be to your MVNO project in terms of duration, cost, quality, or any other important areas of the MVNO project?

# 2.7 Assumption and Constraint Log: MVNO

201. Was the document/deliverable developed per the appropriate or required standards (for example, Institute of Electrical and Electronics Engineers standards)?

202. Security analysis has access to information that is sanitized?

203. Does the system design reflect the requirements?

204. What would you gain if you spent time working to improve this process?

205. Can the requirements be traced to the appropriate components of the solution, as well as test scripts?

206. Does the plan conform to standards?

207. Are there processes defining how software will be developed including development methods, overall timeline for development, software product standards, and traceability?

208. Does the document/deliverable meet all requirements (for example, statement of work) specific to this deliverable?

209. What do you audit?

210. Are there unnecessary steps that are creating bottlenecks and/or causing people to wait?

211. Is the steering committee active in MVNO project oversight?

212. Contradictory information between different documents?

213. Would known impacts serve as impediments?

214. What threats might prevent you from getting there?

215. Have MVNO project management standards and procedures been established and documented?

216. What do you log?

217. Violation trace: why ?

218. Is staff trained on the software technologies that are being used on the MVNO project?

219. After observing execution of process, is it in compliance with the documented Plan?

220. When can log be discarded?

# 2.8 Work Breakdown Structure: MVNO

221. Do you need another level?

222. Why would you develop a Work Breakdown Structure?

223. Is the work breakdown structure (wbs) defined and is the scope of the MVNO project clear with assigned deliverable owners?

224. Can you make it?

225. How will you and your MVNO project team define the MVNO projects scope and work breakdown structure?

226. What has to be done?

227. What is the probability that the MVNO project duration will exceed xx weeks?

228. Why is it useful?

229. How far down?

230. Who has to do it?

231. Is it a change in scope?

232. How big is a work-package?

233. How much detail?

234. How many levels?

235. When do you stop?

236. When does it have to be done?

237. Where does it take place?

238. What is the probability of completing the MVNO project in less that xx days?

239. When would you develop a Work Breakdown Structure?

240. Is it still viable?

# 2.9 WBS Dictionary: MVNO

241. How detailed should a MVNO project get?

242. What should you drop in order to add something new?

243. Are internal budgets for authorized, and not priced changes based on the contractors resource plan for accomplishing the work?

244. Do work packages reflect the actual way in which the work will be done and are they meaningful products or management-oriented subdivisions of a higher level element of work?

245. Should you have a test for each code module?

246. Are records maintained to show how undistributed budgets are controlled?

247. Are the responsibilities and authorities of each of the above organizational elements or managers clearly defined?

248. Does the contractors system provide for accurate cost accumulation and assignment to control accounts in a manner consistent with the budgets using recognized acceptable costing techniques?

249. All cwbs elements specified for external reporting?

250. Are the procedures for identifying indirect costs

to incurring organizations, indirect cost pools, and allocating the costs from the pools to the contracts formally documented?

251. Does the contractors system provide unit costs, equivalent unit or lot costs in terms of labor, material, other direct, and indirect costs?

252. Is authorization of budgets in excess of the contract budget base controlled formally and done with the full knowledge and recognition of the procuring activity?

253. Detailed schedules which support control account and work package start and completion dates/events?

254. Are indirect costs accumulated for comparison with the corresponding budgets?

255. Are procedures established to prevent changes to the contract budget base other than the already stated authorized by contractual action?

256. Identify potential or actual overruns and underruns?

257. Does the contractor have procedures which permit identification of recurring or non-recurring costs as necessary?

258. Changes in the current direct and MVNO projected base?

# 2.10 Schedule Management Plan: MVNO

259. Have the procedures for identifying budget variances been followed?

260. What does a valid Schedule look like?

261. Are vendor contract reports, reviews and visits conducted periodically?

262. Are software metrics formally captured, analyzed and used as a basis for other MVNO project estimates?

263. Is there a formal set of procedures supporting Issues Management?

264. Are decisions captured in a decisions log?

265. Were the budget estimates reasonable?

266. Has a quality assurance plan been developed for the MVNO project?

267. Time for overtime?

268. Cost / benefit analysis?

269. Do all stakeholders know how to access this repository and where to find the MVNO project documentation?

270. Are the MVNO project plans updated on a

frequent basis?

271. Is there a procedure for management, control and release of schedule margin?

272. Are tasks tracked by hours?

273. Do MVNO project managers participating in the MVNO project know the MVNO projects true status first hand?

274. What tools and techniques will be used to estimate activity durations?

275. Are milestone deliverables effectively tracked and compared to MVNO project plan?

276. Has the budget been baselined?

277. What happens if a warning is triggered?

# 2.11 Activity List: MVNO

278. What is the probability the MVNO project can be completed in xx weeks?

279. How difficult will it be to do specific activities on this MVNO project?

280. What are the critical bottleneck activities?

281. Is there anything planned that does not need to be here?

282. What will be performed?

283. What are you counting on?

284. Is infrastructure setup part of your MVNO project?

285. How should ongoing costs be monitored to try to keep the MVNO project within budget?

286. What is the total time required to complete the MVNO project if no delays occur?

287. What went well?

288. Who will perform the work?

289. For other activities, how much delay can be tolerated?

290. Where will it be performed?

291. What went wrong?

292. How can the MVNO project be displayed graphically to better visualize the activities?

293. What did not go as well?

294. How will it be performed?

295. When will the work be performed?

296. How detailed should a MVNO project get?

# 2.12 Activity Attributes: MVNO

297. Were there other ways you could have organized the data to achieve similar results?

298. Where else does it apply?

299. Why?

300. What is the general pattern here?

301. Are the required resources available or need to be acquired?

302. What is missing?

303. How difficult will it be to complete specific activities on this MVNO project?

304. How many resources do you need to complete the work scope within a limit of X number of days?

305. Activity: what is In the Bag?

306. Are the required resources available?

307. Is there a trend during the year?

308. How else could the items be grouped?

309. What conclusions/generalizations can you draw from this?

310. Does your organization of the data change its

meaning?

311. Have constraints been applied to the start and finish milestones for the phases?

312. Do you feel very comfortable with your prediction?

313. How many days do you need to complete the work scope with a limit of X number of resources?

## 2.13 Milestone List: MVNO

314. How soon can the activity start?

315. Obstacles faced?

316. Milestone pages should display the UserID of the person who added the milestone. Does a report or query exist that provides this audit information?

317. It is to be a narrative text providing the crucial aspects of your MVNO project proposal answering what, who, how, when and where?

318. Vital contracts and partners?

319. What would happen if a delivery of material was one week late?

320. Usps (unique selling points)?

321. Can you derive how soon can the whole MVNO project finish?

322. Describe the concept of the technology, product or service that will be or has been developed. How will it be used?

323. Reliability of data, plan predictability?

324. Sustainable financial backing?

325. Do you foresee any technical risks or developmental challenges?

326. Who will manage the MVNO project on a day-to-day basis?

327. When will the MVNO project be complete?

328. Effects on core activities, distraction?

329. Global influences?

## 2.14 Network Diagram: MVNO

330. What activities must occur simultaneously with this activity?

331. What job or jobs precede it?

332. What is the lowest cost to complete this MVNO project in xx weeks?

333. What are the Major Administrative Issues?

334. Where do you schedule uncertainty time?

335. What are the Key Success Factors?

336. Are the gantt chart and/or network diagram updated periodically and used to assess the overall MVNO project timetable?

337. What activity must be completed immediately before this activity can start?

338. How confident can you be in your milestone dates and the delivery date?

339. What to do and When?

340. Which type of network diagram allows you to depict four types of dependencies?

341. What can be done concurrently?

342. What job or jobs could run concurrently?

343. Planning: who, how long, what to do?

344. What job or jobs follow it?

345. What is the completion time?

346. If x is long, what would be the completion time if you break x into two parallel parts of y weeks and z weeks?

347. Will crashing x weeks return more in benefits than it costs?

# 2.15 Activity Resource Requirements: MVNO

348. Anything else?

349. When does monitoring begin?

350. How do you handle petty cash?

351. What are constraints that you might find during the Human Resource Planning process?

352. How many signatures do you require on a check and does this match what is in your policy and procedures?

353. Are there unresolved issues that need to be addressed?

354. Why do you do that?

355. Do you use tools like decomposition and rolling-wave planning to produce the activity list and other outputs?

356. Organizational Applicability?

357. Other support in specific areas?

358. Which logical relationship does the PDM use most often?

359. What is the Work Plan Standard?

## 2.16 Resource Breakdown Structure: MVNO

360. Who will use the system?

361. Which resources should be in the resource pool?

362. Who is allowed to perform which functions?

363. How should the information be delivered?

364. Why time management?

365. What is each stakeholders desired outcome for the MVNO project?

366. Who delivers the information?

367. Why is this important?

368. Why do you do it?

369. How difficult will it be to do specific activities on this MVNO project?

370. Is predictive resource analysis being done?

371. What is the difference between % Complete and % work?

372. What defines a successful MVNO project?

373. Changes based on input from stakeholders?

374. Goals for the MVNO project. What is each stakeholders desired outcome for the MVNO project?

# 2.17 Activity Duration Estimates: MVNO

375. Are adjustments implemented to correct or prevent defects?

376. What is the BEST thing for the MVNO project manager to do?

377. Are MVNO project activities decomposed into manageable components to ensure expected management control?

378. What are some general rules of thumb for deciding if cost variance, schedule variance, cost performance index, and schedule performance index numbers are good or bad?

379. What are the main processes included in MVNO project quality management?

380. What tasks must follow this task?

381. Is a contract developed which obligates the seller and the buyer?

382. What tasks must precede this task?

383. Are procedures followed to ensure information is available to stakeholders in a timely manner?

384. Are tools and techniques defined for gathering, integrating and distributing MVNO project outputs?

385. Will additional funds be needed for hardware or software?

386. What is earned value?

387. How can you use Microsoft MVNO project and Excel to assist in MVNO project risk management?

388. What is wrong with this scenario?

389. Is earned value analysis completed to assess MVNO project performance?

390. How many different communications channels does a MVNO project team with six people have?

391. What is pmp certification, and why do you think the number of people earning it has grown so much in the past ten years?

392. Account for the make-or-buy process and how to perform the financial calculations involved in the process. What are the main types of contracts if you do decide to outsource?

# 2.18 Duration Estimating Worksheet: MVNO

393. What is your role?

394. Define the work as completely as possible. What work will be included in the MVNO project?

395. What is cost and MVNO project cost management?

396. What questions do you have?

397. What is the total time required to complete the MVNO project if no delays occur?

398. Value pocket identification & quantification what are value pockets?

399. Is this operation cost effective?

400. Is the MVNO project responsive to community need?

401. Will the MVNO project collaborate with the local community and leverage resources?

402. Small or large MVNO project?

403. How can the MVNO project be displayed graphically to better visualize the activities?

404. Does the MVNO project provide innovative ways

for stakeholders to overcome obstacles or deliver better outcomes?

405. Is a construction detail attached (to aid in explanation)?

406. Done before proceeding with this activity or what can be done concurrently?

407. How should ongoing costs be monitored to try to keep the MVNO project within budget?

408. When do the individual activities need to start and finish?

409. Why estimate time and cost?

410. When does your organization expect to be able to complete it?

# 2.19 Project Schedule: MVNO

411. Are key risk mitigation strategies added to the MVNO project schedule?

412. How can you fix it?

413. Verify that the update is accurate. Are all remaining durations correct?

414. It allows the MVNO project to be delivered on schedule. How Do you Use Schedules?

415. Is the structure for tracking the MVNO project schedule well defined and assigned to a specific individual?

416. What is MVNO project management?

417. How can you address that situation?

418. Month MVNO project take?

419. What is risk management?

420. Change management required?

421. Was the MVNO project schedule reviewed by all stakeholders and formally accepted?

422. How detailed should a MVNO project get?

423. Meet requirements?

424. Why is this particularly bad?

425. What is the difference?

426. How can slack be negative?

427. If there are any qualifying green components to this MVNO project, what portion of the total MVNO project cost is green?

428. Have all MVNO project delays been adequately accounted for, communicated to all stakeholders and adjustments made in overall MVNO project schedule?

# 2.20 Cost Management Plan: MVNO

429. Are MVNO project contact logs kept up to date?

430. Is there an approved case?

431. Were MVNO project team members involved in detailed estimating and scheduling?

432. Best practices implementation – How will change management be applied to this MVNO project?

433. Have all unresolved risks been documented?

434. Are MVNO project leaders committed to this MVNO project full time?

435. Are risk triggers captured?

436. Cost tracking and performance analysis – How will cost tracking and performance analysis be accomplished?

437. Is there a formal set of procedures supporting Stakeholder Management?

438. Are trade-offs between accepting the risk and mitigating the risk identified?

439. Is the communication plan being followed?

440. Contractors scope – how will contractors scope be defined when contracts are let?

441. Has a capability assessment been conducted?

442. Is the MVNO project schedule available for all MVNO project team members to review?

443. Has the MVNO project scope been baselined?

444. Are action items captured and managed?

445. Has your organization readiness assessment been conducted?

446. Alignment to strategic goals & objectives?

447. Risk rating?

# 2.21 Activity Cost Estimates: MVNO

448. What is MVNO project cost management?

449. What makes a good expected result statement?

450. What is the activity recast of the budget?

451. What are the audit requirements?

452. How do you do activity recasts?

453. Is costing method consistent with study goals?

454. How do you treat administrative costs in the activity inventory?

455. Where can you get activity reports?

456. Did the consultant work with local staff to develop local capacity?

457. Were sponsors and decision makers available when needed outside regularly scheduled meetings?

458. Who determines the quality and expertise of contractors?

459. Does the estimator have experience?

460. What procedures are put in place regarding bidding and cost comparisons, if any?

461. What is your organizations history in doing

similar tasks?

462. What communication items need improvement?

463. Who determines when the contractor is paid?

464. Will you need to provide essential services information about activities?

465. Does the activity rely on a common set of tools to carry it out?

466. Why do you manage cost?

467. How do you change activities?

# 2.22 Cost Estimating Worksheet: MVNO

468. What costs are to be estimated?

469. What happens to any remaining funds not used?

470. What can be included?

471. What info is needed?

472. What additional MVNO project(s) could be initiated as a result of this MVNO project?

473. What is the purpose of estimating?

474. Identify the timeframe necessary to monitor progress and collect data to determine how the selected measure has changed?

475. Who is best positioned to know and assist in identifying corresponding factors?

476. Can a trend be established from historical performance data on the selected measure and are the criteria for using trend analysis or forecasting methods met?

477. Is the MVNO project responsive to community need?

478. How will the results be shared and to whom?

479. Will the MVNO project collaborate with the local community and leverage resources?

480. Ask: are others positioned to know, are others credible, and will others cooperate?

481. Is it feasible to establish a control group arrangement?

482. Does the MVNO project provide innovative ways for stakeholders to overcome obstacles or deliver better outcomes?

483. What will others want?

484. What is the estimated labor cost today based upon this information?

# 2.23 Cost Baseline: MVNO

485. How long are you willing to wait before you find out were late?

486. What is the consequence?

487. On budget?

488. Has the documentation relating to operation and maintenance of the product(s) or service(s) been delivered to, and accepted by, operations management?

489. Where do changes come from?

490. Does the suggested change request represent a desired enhancement to the products functionality?

491. Pcs for your new business. what would the life cycle costs be?

492. What strengths do you have?

493. Verify business objectives. Are others appropriate, and well-articulated?

494. Have the resources used by the MVNO project been reassigned to other units or MVNO projects?

495. Has the MVNO project (or MVNO project phase) been evaluated against each objective established in the product description and Integrated MVNO project Plan?

496. Will the MVNO project fail if the change request is not executed?

497. When should cost estimates be developed?

498. What deliverables come first?

499. On time?

500. Have the actual milestone completion dates been compared to the approved schedule?

501. Is the requested change request a result of changes in other MVNO project(s)?

502. Are procedures defined by which the cost baseline may be changed?

## 2.24 Quality Management Plan: MVNO

503. How is staff trained on the recording of field notes?

504. Show/provide copy of procedures for taking field notes?

505. Diagrams and tables to account for complex concepts and increase overall readability?

506. What does it do for you (or to me)?

507. How are calibration records kept?

508. How do you ensure that your sampling methods and procedures meet your data quality objectives?

509. How relevant is this attribute to this MVNO project or audit?

510. Were the right locations/samples tested for the right parameters?

511. How do you decide what information to record?

512. How do your action plans support the strategic objectives?

513. If it is out of compliance, should the process be amended or should the Plan be amended?

514. Was trending evident between audits?

515. How does your organization decide what to measure?

516. How does your organization measure customer satisfaction/dissatisfaction?

517. With the five whys method, the team considers why the issue being explored occurred. do others then take that initial answer and ask why?

518. Is there a procedure for this process?

519. How many MVNO project staff does this specific process affect?

520. Written by multiple authors and in multiple writing styles?

521. What are your organizations current levels and trends for the already stated measures related to financial and marketplace performance?

522. Where do you focus?

# 2.25 Quality Metrics: MVNO

523. What if the biggest risk to your business were the already stated people who do not complain?

524. Was review conducted per standard protocols?

525. How effective are your security tests?

526. Has it met internal or external standards?

527. Can visual measures help you to filter visualizations of interest?

528. Should a modifier be included?

529. How do you measure?

530. Are there already quality metrics available that detect nonlinear embeddings and trends similar to the users perception?

531. What makes a visualization memorable?

532. Were quality attributes reported?

533. Was material distributed on time?

534. What forces exist that would cause them to change?

535. What is the benchmark?

536. If the defect rate during testing is substantially

higher than that of the previous release (or a similar product), then ask: Did you plan for and actually improve testing effectiveness?

537. Where did complaints, returns and warranty claims come from?

538. Which data do others need in one place to target areas of improvement?

539. When is the security analysis testing complete?

540. Was the overall quality better or worse than previous products?

541. Filter visualizations of interest?

542. What do you measure?

## 2.26 Process Improvement Plan: MVNO

543. Has the time line required to move measurement results from the points of collection to databases or users been established?

544. What personnel are the coaches for your initiative?

545. Have storage and access mechanisms and procedures been determined?

546. Modeling current processes is great, and will you ever see a return on that investment?

547. What actions are needed to address the problems and achieve the goals?

548. If a process improvement framework is being used, which elements will help the problems and goals listed?

549. Are you making progress on the improvement framework?

550. Does explicit definition of the measures exist?

551. The motive is determined by asking, Why do you want to achieve this goal?

552. Where are you now?

553. Who should prepare the process improvement action plan?

554. Has a process guide to collect the data been developed?

555. Why do you want to achieve the goal?

556. Management commitment at all levels?

557. Where do you want to be?

558. What is quality and how will you ensure it?

559. Are you making progress on the goals?

560. What is the return on investment?

561. Purpose of goal: the motive is determined by asking, why do you want to achieve this goal?

562. Everyone agrees on what process improvement is, right?

# 2.27 Responsibility Assignment Matrix: MVNO

563. Are significant decision points, constraints, and interfaces identified as key milestones?

564. Too many is: do all the identified roles need to be routinely informed or only in exceptional circumstances?

565. Is all contract work included in the CWBS?

566. Authorization to proceed with all authorized work?

567. What do you do when people do not respond?

568. Are people encouraged to bring up issues?

569. When performing is split among two or more roles, is the work clearly defined so that the efforts are coordinated and the communication is clear?

570. What are some important MVNO project communications management tools?

571. Does each role with Accountable responsibility have the authority within your organization to make the required decisions?

572. What expertise is not available in your department?

573. Is accountability placed at the lowest-possible level within the MVNO project so that decisions can be made at that level?

574. What tool can show you individual and group allocations?

575. Is it safe to say you can handle more work or that some tasks you are supposed to do arent worth doing?

576. What do people write/say on status/MVNO project reports?

577. Are material costs reported within the same period as that in which BCWP is earned for that material?

578. What happens when others get pulled for higher priority MVNO projects?

579. Do you need to convince people that its well worth the time and effort?

580. Which MVNO project management knowledge area is least mature?

581. Are too many reports done in writing instead of verbally?

# 2.28 Roles and Responsibilities: MVNO

582. Authority: what areas/MVNO projects in your work do you have the authority to decide upon and act on the already stated decisions?

583. Implementation of actions: Who are the responsible units?

584. Influence: what areas of organizational decision making are you able to influence when you do not have authority to make the final decision?

585. Is there a training program in place for stakeholders covering expectations, roles and responsibilities and any addition knowledge others need to be good stakeholders?

586. Attainable / achievable: the goal is attainable; can you actually accomplish the goal?

587. Are your policies supportive of a culture of quality data?

588. Have you ever been a part of this team?

589. Where are you most strong as a supervisor?

590. What should you do now to prepare yourself for a promotion, increased responsibilities or a different job?

591. Are MVNO project team roles and responsibilities identified and documented?

592. Is feedback clearly communicated and non-judgmental?

593. How well did the MVNO project Team understand the expectations of specific roles and responsibilities?

594. Who is responsible for implementation activities and where will the functions, roles and responsibilities be defined?

595. Does your vision/mission support a culture of quality data?

596. Once the responsibilities are defined for the MVNO project, have the deliverables, roles and responsibilities been clearly communicated to every participant?

597. What should you do now to prepare for your career 5+ years from now?

598. Key conclusions and recommendations: Are conclusions and recommendations relevant and acceptable?

599. Was the expectation clearly communicated?

600. Concern: where are you limited or have no authority, where you can not influence?

601. What should you highlight for improvement?

## 2.29 Human Resource Management Plan: MVNO

602. Have external dependencies been captured in the schedule?

603. How are superior performers differentiated from average performers?

604. Are target dates established for each milestone deliverable?

605. Are internal MVNO project status meetings held at reasonable intervals?

606. Are mitigation strategies identified?

607. Staffing Requirements?

608. Are the MVNO project plans updated on a frequent basis?

609. Have key stakeholders been identified?

610. Is there a formal process for updating the MVNO project baseline?

611. What were things that you did very well and want to do the same again on the next MVNO project?

612. Sensitivity analysis?

613. Have all necessary approvals been obtained?

614. Is it standard practice to formally commit stakeholders to the MVNO project via agreements?

615. Are quality metrics defined?

616. Are changes in deliverable commitments agreed to by all affected groups & individuals?

617. Are procurement deliverables arriving on time and to specification?

618. Are the key elements of a MVNO project Charter present?

## 2.30 Communications Management Plan: MVNO

619. What is the stakeholders level of authority?

620. Do you prepare stakeholder engagement plans?

621. Is the stakeholder role recognized by your organization?

622. Why manage stakeholders?

623. How much time does it take to do it?

624. How do you manage communications?

625. How were corresponding initiatives successful?

626. Who have you worked with in past, similar initiatives?

627. What is the political influence?

628. Do you feel a register helps?

629. Is there an important stakeholder who is actively opposed and will not receive messages?

630. Who did you turn to if you had questions?

631. What steps can you take for a positive relationship?

632. Who to learn from?

633. Will messages be directly related to the release strategy or phases of the MVNO project?

634. Who is involved as you identify stakeholders?

635. Who are the members of the governing body?

636. Which stakeholders can influence others?

637. Can you think of other people who might have concerns or interests?

# 2.31 Risk Management Plan: MVNO

638. Is the customer willing to establish rapid communication links with the developer?

639. What are the cost, schedule and resource impacts of avoiding the risk?

640. What should be done with non-critical risks?

641. How are risk analvsis and prioritization performed?

642. Prioritized components/features?

643. Is the customer technically sophisticated in the product area?

644. Where are you confronted with risks during the business phases?

645. Can the MVNO project proceed without assuming the risk?

646. Is the technology to be built new to your organization?

647. Risk documentation: what reporting formats and processes will be used for risk management activities?

648. Are the required plans included, such as nonstructural flood risk management plans?

649. How much risk can you tolerate?

650. How much risk protection can you afford?

651. Do you have a consistent repeatable process that is actually used?

652. What will drive change?

653. What risks are tracked?

654. Are people attending meetings and doing work?

655. If you can not fix it, how do you do it differently?

656. What are the chances the event will occur?

# 2.32 Risk Register: MVNO

657. Are there any knock-on effects/impact on any of the other areas?

658. Is further information required before making a decision?

659. Risk probability and impact: how will the probabilities and impacts of risk items be assessed?

660. Who is accountable?

661. What is your current and future risk profile?

662. Amongst the action plans and recommendations that you have to introduce are there some that could stop or delay the overall program?

663. Are there any gaps in the evidence?

664. What could prevent you delivering on the strategic program objectives and what is being done to mitigate corresponding issues?

665. What is the appropriate level of risk management for this MVNO project?

666. When is it going to be done?

667. Are there other alternative controls that could be implemented?

668. How are risks identified?

669. Assume the event happens, what is the Most Likely impact?

670. Methodology: how will risk management be performed on this MVNO project?

671. Which key risks have ineffective responses or outstanding improvement actions?

672. User involvement: do you have the right users?

673. What should you do now?

674. Contingency actions - planned actions to reduce the immediate seriousness of the risk when it does occur. What should you do when?

675. Who is going to do it?

# 2.33 Probability and Impact Assessment: MVNO

676. Can it be enlarged by drawing people from other areas of your organization?

677. What things might go wrong?

678. What things are likely to change?

679. Do benefits and chances of success outweigh potential damage if success is not attained?

680. What is the level of experience available with your organization?

681. Who will be responsible for a slippage?

682. How risk averse are you?

683. What should be the gestation period for the MVNO project with specific technology?

684. What would be the effect of slippage?

685. Can you avoid altogether some things that might go wrong?

686. What are the tools and techniques used in managing the challenges faced?

687. Are trained personnel, including supervisors and MVNO project managers, available to handle such a

large MVNO project?

688. Do you have a mechanism for managing change?

689. How much risk do others need to take?

690. How do the products attain the specifications?

691. What is the MVNO project managers level of commitment and professionalism?

692. Does the software interface with new or unproven hardware or unproven vendor products?

693. How is the MVNO project going to be managed?

694. Are tools for analysis and design available?

695. Can the MVNO project proceed without assuming the risk?

# 2.34 Probability and Impact Matrix: MVNO

696. Is the present organizational structure for handling the MVNO project sufficient?

697. What can you use the analyzed risks for?

698. Is the number of people on the MVNO project team adequate to do the job?

699. Are compilers and code generators available and suitable for the product to be built?

700. What will be the impact or consequence if the risk occurs?

701. My MVNO project leader has suddenly left your organization, what do you do?

702. What would be the best solution?

703. Who are the owners?

704. Have staff received necessary training?

705. Are enough people available?

706. What can possibly go wrong?

707. Number of users of the product?

708. How is the MVNO project going to be managed?

709. Have you ascribed a level of confidence to every critical technical objective?

710. Mandated delivery date?

711. What can go wrong?

712. What is the likelihood of a breakthrough?

713. What will be the environmental impact of the MVNO project?

714. Do you know the order of planning yet?

# 2.35 Risk Data Sheet: MVNO

715. What was measured?

716. What do you know?

717. Has the most cost-effective solution been chosen?

718. How can it happen?

719. Type of risk identified?

720. During work activities could hazards exist?

721. Whom do you serve (customers)?

722. If it happens, what are the consequences?

723. How can hazards be reduced?

724. Are new hazards created?

725. What is the environment within which you operate (social trends, economic, community values, broad based participation, national directions etc.)?

726. What can you do?

727. What is the likelihood of it happening?

728. What do people affected think about the need for, and practicality of preventive measures?

729. Is the data sufficiently specified in terms of the type of failure being analyzed, and its frequency or probability?

730. What are you weak at and therefore need to do better?

731. Who has a vested interest in how you perform as your organization (our stakeholders)?

732. Potential for recurrence?

733. What actions can be taken to eliminate or remove risk?

734. How do you handle product safely?

## 2.36 Procurement Management Plan: MVNO

735. Was an original risk assessment/risk management plan completed?

736. Are software metrics formally captured, analyzed and used as a basis for other MVNO project estimates?

737. Are internal MVNO project status meetings held at reasonable intervals?

738. Are meeting minutes captured and sent out after meetings?

739. Is it standard practice to formally commit stakeholders to the MVNO project via agreements?

740. Is there an on-going process in place to monitor MVNO project risks?

741. Have reserves been created to address risks?

742. Is there a set of procedures defining the scope, procedures, and deliverables defining quality control?

743. What are things that you need to improve?

744. Has the MVNO project scope been baselined?

745. Are quality inspections and review activities listed in the MVNO project schedule(s)?

746. Public engagement – did you get it right?

747. Are meeting objectives identified for each meeting?

748. Is the steering committee active in MVNO project oversight?

749. Are updated MVNO project time & resource estimates reasonable based on the current MVNO project stage?

750. Is the MVNO project sponsor clearly communicating the business case or rationale for why this MVNO project is needed?

751. What types of contracts will be used?

752. Are written status reports provided on a designated frequent basis?

# 2.37 Source Selection Criteria: MVNO

753. When and what information can be considered with offerors regarding past performance?

754. What are the most common types of rating systems?

755. Comparison of each offers prices to the estimated prices -are there significant differences?

756. What information is to be provided and when should it be provided?

757. How should the solicitation aspects regarding past performance be structured?

758. How is past performance evaluated?

759. Is experience evaluated?

760. Do you have designated specific forms or worksheets?

761. Do proposed hours support content and schedule?

762. What is the effect of the debriefing schedule on potential protests?

763. How can business terms and conditions be improved to yield more effective price competition?

764. What will you use to capture evaluation and

subsequent documentation?

765. Have all evaluators been trained?

766. If the costs are normalized, please account for how the normalization is conducted. Is a cost realism analysis used?

767. What should clarifications include?

768. Who is entitled to a debriefing?

769. How and when do you enter into MVNO project Procurement Management?

770. Has all proposal data been loaded?

771. How will you decide an evaluators write up is sufficient?

772. Can you prevent comparison of proposals?

# 2.38 Stakeholder Management Plan: MVNO

773. What training requirements are there based upon the required skills and resources?

774. Are cause and effect determined for risks when they occur?

775. Are software metrics formally captured, analyzed and used as a basis for other MVNO project estimates?

776. Why would a customer be interested in a particular product or service?

777. Are metrics used to evaluate and manage Vendors?

778. Are stakeholders aware and supportive of the principles and practices of modern software estimation?

779. Quality assurance overheads?

780. What other teams / processes would be impacted by changes to the current process, and how?

781. Is the quality assurance team identified?

782. Does this include subcontracted development?

783. Who will the report(s) be delivered to?

784. At what point will the MVNO project be closed and what will be done to formally close the MVNO project?

785. Where to get additional help?

786. Are MVNO project team members committed fulltime?

787. Are staff skills known and available for each task?

788. Have the key elements of a coherent MVNO project management strategy been established?

789. Are parking lot items captured?

790. What guidelines or procedures currently exist that must be adhered to (eg departmental accounting procedures)?

## 2.39 Change Management Plan: MVNO

791. Have the approved procedures and policies been published?

792. What provokes organizational change?

793. How can you best frame the message so that it addresses the audiences interests?

794. What relationships will change?

795. How badly can information be misinterpreted?

796. How does the principle of senders and receivers make the MVNO project communications effort more complex?

797. Will a different work structure focus people on what is important?

798. Who should be involved in developing a change management strategy?

799. Does this change represent a completely new process for your organization, or a different application of an existing process?

800. What are the responsibilities assigned to each role?

801. What are you trying to achieve as a result of

communication?

802. What new competencies will be required for the roles?

803. Why is the initiative is being undertaken - What are the business drivers?

804. What processes are in place to manage knowledge about the MVNO project?

805. Has a training need analysis been carried out?

806. What risks may occur upfront, during implementation and after implementation?

807. What are the training strategies?

808. What does a resilient organization look like?

809. Identify the risk and assess the significance and likelihood of it occurring and plan the contingency What risks may occur upfront?

810. Has this been negotiated with the customer and sponsor?

# 3.0 Executing Process Group: MVNO

811. How does a MVNO project life cycle differ from a product life cycle?

812. After how many days will the lease cost be the same as the purchase cost for the equipment?

813. What are the main parts of the scope statement?

814. What are the key components of the MVNO project communications plan?

815. How does MVNO project management relate to other disciplines?

816. Is activity definition the first process involved in MVNO project time management?

817. What business situation is being addressed?

818. Why is it important to determine activity sequencing on MVNO projects?

819. How well defined and documented were the MVNO project management processes you chose to use?

820. Is the MVNO project making progress in helping to achieve the set results?

821. How does the job market and current state of the economy affect human resource management?

822. How could stakeholders negatively impact your MVNO project?

823. What areas were overlooked on this MVNO project?

824. Why should MVNO project managers strive to make jobs look easy?

825. Have operating capacities been created and/or reinforced in partners?

826. When will the MVNO project be done?

827. How can software assist in MVNO project communications?

# 3.1 Team Member Status Report: MVNO

828. How will resource planning be done?

829. Is there evidence that staff is taking a more professional approach toward management of your organizations MVNO projects?

830. When a teams productivity and success depend on collaboration and the efficient flow of information, what generally fails them?

831. Will the staff do training or is that done by a third party?

832. Does your organization have the means (staff, money, contract, etc.) to produce or to acquire the product, good, or service?

833. How much risk is involved?

834. How it is to be done?

835. Are the products of your organizations MVNO projects meeting customers objectives?

836. How does this product, good, or service meet the needs of the MVNO project and your organization as a whole?

837. What specific interest groups do you have in place?

838. Does the product, good, or service already exist within your organization?

839. Why is it to be done?

840. Are your organizations MVNO projects more successful over time?

841. Do you have an Enterprise MVNO project Management Office (EPMO)?

842. The problem with Reward & Recognition Programs is that the truly deserving people all too often get left out. How can you make it practical?

843. Are the attitudes of staff regarding MVNO project work improving?

844. How can you make it practical?

845. What is to be done?

846. Does every department have to have a MVNO project Manager on staff?

## 3.2 Change Request: MVNO

847. Will the change use memory to the extent that other functions will be not have sufficient memory to operate effectively?

848. Will new change requests be acknowledged in a timely manner?

849. How shall the implementation of changes be recorded?

850. What is a Change Request Form?

851. How many times must the change be modified or presented to the change control board before it is approved?

852. Customer acceptance plan how will the customer verify the change has been implemented successfully?

853. Will there be a change request form in use?

854. Should a more thorough impact analysis be conducted?

855. How can you ensure that changes have been made properly?

856. When to submit a change request?

857. Describe how modifications, enhancements, defects and/or deficiencies shall be notified (e.g.

Problem Reports, Change Requests etc) and managed. Detail warranty and/or maintenance periods?

858. What has an inspector to inspect and to check?

859. Are there requirements attributes that are strongly related to the complexity and size?

860. How are the measures for carrying out the change established?

861. How to get changes (code) out in a timely manner?

862. Have all related configuration items been properly updated?

863. How is quality being addressed on the MVNO project?

864. What is the purpose of change control?

865. Are there requirements attributes that can discriminate between high and low reliability?

866. Why control change across the life cycle?

# 3.3 Change Log: MVNO

867. Is the change request open, closed or pending?

868. Is the change request within MVNO project scope?

869. Is the requested change request a result of changes in other MVNO project(s)?

870. Do the described changes impact on the integrity or security of the system?

871. How does this change affect the timeline of the schedule?

872. Does the suggested change request seem to represent a necessary enhancement to the product?

873. Is the change backward compatible without limitations?

874. How does this change affect scope?

875. Is this a mandatory replacement?

876. Is the submitted change a new change or a modification of a previously approved change?

877. When was the request approved?

878. How does this relate to the standards developed for specific business processes?

879. When was the request submitted?

880. Who initiated the change request?

881. Will the MVNO project fail if the change request is not executed?

# 3.4 Decision Log: MVNO

882. What eDiscovery problem or issue did your organization set out to fix or make better?

883. How do you know when you are achieving it?

884. Behaviors; what are guidelines that the team has identified that will assist them with getting the most out of team meetings?

885. Meeting purpose; why does this team meet?

886. Linked to original objective?

887. Is your opponent open to a non-traditional workflow, or will it likely challenge anything you do?

888. It becomes critical to track and periodically revisit both operational effectiveness; Are you noticing all that you need to, and are you interpreting what you see effectively?

889. What are the cost implications?

890. How do you define success?

891. What is the average size of your matters in an applicable measurement?

892. How effective is maintaining the log at facilitating organizational learning?

893. What was the rationale for the decision?

894. Do strategies and tactics aimed at less than full control reduce the costs of management or simply shift the cost burden?

895. Which variables make a critical difference?

896. Who is the decisionmaker?

897. What alternatives/risks were considered?

898. Decision-making process; how will the team make decisions?

899. How does the use a Decision Support System influence the strategies/tactics or costs?

900. What is your overall strategy for quality control / quality assurance procedures?

901. At what point in time does loss become unacceptable?

# 3.5 Quality Audit: MVNO

902. How does your organization know that its system for managing intellectual property issues is appropriately effective, constructive and fair?

903. How does your organization know that its system for supporting staff research capability is appropriately effective and constructive?

904. How does your organization know that the range and quality of its social and recreational services and facilities are appropriately effective and constructive in meeting the needs of staff?

905. How does your organization know that its staff placements are appropriately effective and constructive in relation to program-related learning outcomes?

906. Can your organization demonstrate exactly how and why results were achieved?

907. How does your organization know that its relationship with its (past) staff is appropriately effective and constructive?

908. Is there a risk that information provided by management may not always be reliable?

909. If your organization thinks it is doing something well, can it prove this?

910. What does the organizarion look for in a Quality

audit?

911. What are you trying to accomplish with this audit?

912. Have the risks associated with the intentions been identified, analyzed and appropriate responses developed?

913. How does your organization know that the support for its staff is appropriately effective and constructive?

914. How does your organization know that its financial management system is appropriately effective and constructive?

915. How well do you think your organization engages with the outside community?

916. How does your organization know that its system for ensuring a positive organizational climate is appropriately effective and constructive?

917. Does everyone know what they are supposed to be doing, how and why?

918. Is there a written corporate quality policy?

919. Are all records associated with the reconditioning of a device maintained for a minimum of two years after the sale or disposal of the last device within a lot of merchandise?

920. Does the suppliers quality system have a written procedure for corrective action when a defect occurs?

921. Has a written procedure been established to identify devices during all stages of receipt, reconditioning, distribution and installation so that mix-ups are prevented?

# 3.6 Team Directory: MVNO

922. Decisions: what could be done better to improve the quality of the constructed product?

923. Who are your stakeholders (customers, sponsors, end users, team members)?

924. Where should the information be distributed?

925. Do purchase specifications and configurations match requirements?

926. What needs to be communicated?

927. Where will the product be used and/or delivered or built when appropriate?

928. Process decisions: are contractors adequately prosecuting the work?

929. Is construction on schedule?

930. Process decisions: do invoice amounts match accepted work in place?

931. Timing: when do the effects of communication take place?

932. How will the team handle changes?

933. Who are the Team Members?

934. Process decisions: how well was task order work

performed?

935. Process decisions: is work progressing on schedule and per contract requirements?

936. Process decisions: are all start-up, turn over and close out requirements of the contract satisfied?

937. Process decisions: which organizational elements and which individuals will be assigned management functions?

938. Who will report MVNO project status to all stakeholders?

939. How will you accomplish and manage the objectives?

940. Who will talk to the customer?

# 3.7 Team Operating Agreement: MVNO

941. Is compensation based on team and individual performance?

942. Do you vary your voice pace, tone and pitch to engage participants and gain involvement?

943. What are the current caseload numbers in the unit?

944. The method to be used in the decision making process; Will it be consensus, majority rule, or the supervisor having the final say?

945. Do you post any action items, due dates, and responsibilities on the team website?

946. Must your members collaborate successfully to complete MVNO projects?

947. To whom do you deliver your services?

948. Are there differences in access to communication and collaboration technology based on team member location?

949. Do you use a parking lot for any items that are important and outside of the agenda?

950. Methodologies: how will key team processes be implemented, such as training, research, work

deliverable production, review and approval processes, knowledge management, and meeting procedures?

951. Do you listen for voice tone and word choice to understand the meaning behind words?

952. Do you brief absent members after they view meeting notes or listen to a recording?

953. What is the number of cases currently teamed?

954. How does teaming fit in with overall organizational goals and meet organizational needs?

955. How will you divide work equitably?

956. How will you resolve conflict efficiently and respectfully?

957. Are there more than two functional areas represented by your team?

958. Are there the right people on your team?

959. Have you established procedures that team members can follow to work effectively together, such as a team operating agreement?

960. Do team members need to frequently communicate as a full group to make timely decisions?

# 3.8 Team Performance Assessment: MVNO

961. Where to from here?

962. Effects of crew composition on crew performance: Does the whole equal the sum of its parts?

963. What are teams?

964. Does more radicalness mean more perceived benefits?

965. To what degree are fresh input and perspectives systematically caught and added (for example, through information and analysis, new members, and senior sponsors)?

966. To what degree can all members engage in open and interactive considerations?

967. What are you doing specifically to develop the leaders around you?

968. To what degree can team members frequently and easily communicate with one another?

969. To what degree are staff involved as partners in the improvement process?

970. To what degree do team members articulate the teams work approach?

971. What is method variance?

972. If you have criticized someones work for method variance in your role as reviewer, what was the circumstance?

973. Individual task proficiency and team process behavior: what is important for team functioning?

974. How do you manage human resources?

975. Delaying market entry: how long is too long?

976. To what degree is the team cognizant of small wins to be celebrated along the way?

977. Lack of method variance in self-reported affect and perceptions at work: Reality or artifact?

978. To what degree can team members vigorously define the teams purpose in considerations with others who are not part of the functioning team?

979. To what degree do team members frequently explore the teams purpose and its implications?

980. Social categorization and intergroup behaviour: Does minimal intergroup discrimination make social identity more positive?

# 3.9 Team Member Performance Assessment: MVNO

981. How is assessment information achieved, stored?

982. How is your organizations Strategic Management System tied to performance measurement?

983. What is used as a basis for instructional decisions?

984. What are the evaluation strategies (e.g., reaction, learning, behavior, results) used. What evaluation results did you have?

985. Are assessment validation activities performed?

986. Are any governance changes sufficient to impact achievement?

987. How will you identify your Team Leaders?

988. Is it critical or vital to the job?

989. What kinds of performance factors / elements do you use?

990. Who should attend?

991. What is the target group for instruction (e.g., individual and collective or small team instruction)?

992. What are best practices for delivering and

developing training evaluations to maximize the benefits of leveraging emerging technologies?

993. To what degree are sub-teams possible or necessary?

994. What types of learning are targeted (e.g., cognitive, affective, psychomotor, procedural)?

995. How should adaptive assessments be implemented?

996. What resources do you need?

997. How are performance measures and associated incentives developed?

998. How does your team work together?

999. How do you make use of research?

# 3.10 Issue Log: MVNO

1000. How do you reply to this question; you am new here and managing this major program. How do you suggest you build your network?

1001. What effort will a change need?

1002. Are the MVNO project issues uniquely identified, including to which product they refer?

1003. What is a change?

1004. What does the stakeholder need from the team?

1005. Who needs to know and how much?

1006. What approaches to you feel are the best ones to use?

1007. How were past initiatives successful?

1008. Do you often overlook a key stakeholder or stakeholder group?

1009. Why do you manage human resources?

1010. Which team member will work with each stakeholder?

1011. Why do you manage communications?

1012. Why multiple evaluators?

1013. Are they needed?

1014. Who do you turn to if you have questions?

1015. Are the stakeholders getting the information they need, are they consulted, are concerns addressed?

1016. Is the issue log kept in a safe place?

# 4.0 Monitoring and Controlling Process Group: MVNO

1017. Based on your MVNO project communication management plan, what worked well?

1018. How well did the chosen processes fit the needs of the MVNO project?

1019. Mitigate. what will you do to minimize the impact should a risk event occur?

1020. What do they need to know about the MVNO project?

1021. What departments are involved in its daily operation?

1022. Is the verbiage used appropriate and understandable?

1023. What were things that you did very well and want to do the same again on the next MVNO project?

1024. Propriety: who needs to be involved in the evaluation to be ethical?

1025. What input will you be required to provide the MVNO project team?

1026. How are you doing?

1027. How can you monitor progress?

1028. What areas does the group agree are the biggest success on the MVNO project?

1029. Is there adequate validation on required fields?

1030. What will you do to minimize the impact should a risk event occur?

1031. Is the schedule for the set products being met?

1032. Use: how will they use the information?

1033. Accuracy: what design will lead to accurate information?

1034. What is the expected monetary value of the MVNO project?

# 4.1 Project Performance Report: MVNO

1035. To what degree is the information network consistent with the structure of the formal organization?

1036. To what degree can the team ensure that all members are individually and jointly accountable for the teams purpose, goals, approach, and work-products?

1037. To what degree will team members, individually and collectively, commit time to help themselves and others learn and develop skills?

1038. To what degree do the structures of the formal organization motivate taskrelevant behavior and facilitate task completion?

1039. How is the data used?

1040. To what degree are the teams goals and objectives clear, simple, and measurable?

1041. What is in it for you?

1042. What is the degree to which rules govern information exchange between individuals within your organization?

1043. To what degree does the information network communicate information relevant to the task?

1044. To what degree are the goals realistic?

1045. To what degree are the structures of the formal organization consistent with the behaviors in the informal organization?

1046. To what degree do individual skills and abilities match task demands?

1047. What is the PRS?

1048. To what degree does the teams work approach provide opportunity for members to engage in fact-based problem solving?

1049. What degree are the relative importance and priority of the goals clear to all team members?

1050. Next Steps?

1051. To what degree does the teams work approach provide opportunity for members to engage in open interaction?

1052. To what degree does the informal organization make use of individual resources and meet individual needs?

# 4.2 Variance Analysis: MVNO

1053. Are there externalities from having some customers, even if they are unprofitable in the short run?

1054. There are detailed schedules which support control account and work package start and completion dates/events?

1055. Why are standard cost systems used?

1056. How do you identify potential or actual overruns and underruns?

1057. How does your organization allocate the cost of shared expenses and services?

1058. Does the scheduling system identify in a timely manner the status of work?

1059. What is the actual cost of work performed?

1060. How are material, labor, and overhead standards set?

1061. Who is generally responsible for monitoring and taking action on variances?

1062. What is the performance to date and material commitment?

1063. What is the total budget for the MVNO project (including estimates for authorized and unpriced work)?

1064. Did an existing competitor change strategy?

1065. Are indirect costs charged to the appropriate indirect pools and incurring organization?

1066. Why do variances exist?

1067. Does the contractors system identify work accomplishment against the schedule plan?

1068. Are authorized changes being incorporated in a timely manner?

1069. How have the setting and use of standards changed over time?

1070. Are estimates of costs at completion generated in a rational, consistent manner?

1071. What are the actual costs to date?

1072. Other relevant issues of Variance Analysis -selling price or gross margin?

# 4.3 Earned Value Status: MVNO

1073. Where are your problem areas?

1074. When is it going to finish?

1075. Validation is a process of ensuring that the developed system will actually achieve the stakeholders desired outcomes; Are you building the right product? What do you validate?

1076. Earned value can be used in almost any MVNO project situation and in almost any MVNO project environment. it may be used on large MVNO projects, medium sized MVNO projects, tiny MVNO projects (in cut-down form), complex and simple MVNO projects and in any market sector. some people, of course, know all about earned value, they have used it for years - but perhaps not as effectively as they could have?

1077. How much is it going to cost by the finish?

1078. What is the unit of forecast value?

1079. If earned value management (EVM) is so good in determining the true status of a MVNO project and MVNO project its completion, why is it that hardly any one uses it in information systems related MVNO projects?

1080. Where is evidence-based earned value in your organization reported?

1081. How does this compare with other MVNO projects?

1082. Are you hitting your MVNO projects targets?

1083. Verification is a process of ensuring that the developed system satisfies the stakeholders agreements and specifications; Are you building the product right? What do you verify?

# 4.4 Risk Audit: MVNO

1084. What can you do to manage outcomes?

1085. Are procedures developed to respond to foreseeable emergencies and communicated to all involved?

1086. Does your organization meet the terms of any contracts with which it is involved?

1087. Does the customer understand the process?

1088. Has an event time line been developed?

1089. Are all managers or operators of the facility or equipment competent or qualified?

1090. Does your organization have a register of insurance policies detailing all current insurance policies?

1091. Are requirements fully understood by the team and customers?

1092. Are risk management strategies documented?

1093. Is all required equipment available?

1094. What can be measured?

1095. Do you have written and signed agreements/ contracts in place for each paid staff member?

1096. What compliance systems do you have in place to address quality, errors, and outcomes?

1097. Is there a screening process that will ensure all participants have the fitness and skills required to safely participate?

1098. Do you have financial policies and procedures in place to guide officers of your organization/treasurer/ general members?

1099. To what extent are auditors influenced by the business risk assessment in the audit process, and how can auditors create more effective mental models to more fully examine contradictory evidence?

1100. What are the strategic implications with clients when auditors focus audit resources based on business-level risks?

1101. Are team members trained in the use of the tools?

1102. Mitigation -how can you avoid the risk?

# 4.5 Contractor Status Report: MVNO

1103. What was the overall budget or estimated cost?

1104. Who can list a MVNO project as organization experience, your organization or a previous employee of your organization?

1105. How is risk transferred?

1106. Are there contractual transfer concerns?

1107. Describe how often regular updates are made to the proposed solution. Are corresponding regular updates included in the standard maintenance plan?

1108. How does the proposed individual meet each requirement?

1109. What was the actual budget or estimated cost for your organizations services?

1110. What process manages the contracts?

1111. What was the budget or estimated cost for your organizations services?

1112. If applicable; describe your standard schedule for new software version releases. Are new software version releases included in the standard maintenance plan?

1113. What are the minimum and optimal bandwidth requirements for the proposed soluiton?

1114. How long have you been using the services?

1115. What is the average response time for answering a support call?

1116. What was the final actual cost?

# 4.6 Formal Acceptance: MVNO

1117. Does it do what client said it would?

1118. Did the MVNO project achieve its MOV?

1119. Did the MVNO project manager and team act in a professional and ethical manner?

1120. How does your team plan to obtain formal acceptance on your MVNO project?

1121. How well did the team follow the methodology?

1122. What function(s) does it fill or meet?

1123. Was the MVNO project managed well?

1124. What are the requirements against which to test, Who will execute?

1125. Is formal acceptance of the MVNO project product documented and distributed?

1126. Was the client satisfied with the MVNO project results?

1127. Do you buy-in installation services?

1128. What lessons were learned about your MVNO project management methodology?

1129. What can you do better next time?

1130. What was done right?

1131. Who would use it?

1132. Was the sponsor/customer satisfied?

1133. Who supplies data?

1134. Was the MVNO project goal achieved?

1135. What is the Acceptance Management Process?

1136. Have all comments been addressed?

# 5.0 Closing Process Group: MVNO

1137. What level of risk does the proposed budget represent to the MVNO project?

1138. Was the user/client satisfied with the end product?

1139. Did the delivered product meet the specified requirements and goals of the MVNO project?

1140. What was learned?

1141. Can the lesson learned be replicated?

1142. Is there a clear cause and effect between the activity and the lesson learned?

1143. What can you do better next time, and what specific actions can you take to improve?

1144. Did you do things well?

1145. Did the MVNO project team have enough people to execute the MVNO project plan?

1146. How well did you do?

1147. What could have been improved?

1148. Did the MVNO project team have the right skills?

1149. What is the MVNO project name and date of

completion?

1150. Is this a follow-on to a previous MVNO project?

1151. Were the outcomes different from the already stated planned?

1152. How well did the chosen processes produce the expected results?

1153. What areas does the group agree are the biggest success on the MVNO project?

# 5.1 Procurement Audit: MVNO

1154. If an electronic auction or a dynamic purchasing system was used, did the tender documents specify details on access to information, electronic equipment used and connection specifications?

1155. Has your organization procedures in place to monitor the input of experts employed to assist the procurement function?

1156. Where required, were candidates registered as approved contractors, suppliers or service providers or certified by relevant bodies?

1157. Are regulations on taxes, fees, duties, excises, tariffs etc. not impeding (international) competition?

1158. Are checks safeguarded against theft, loss, or misuse?

1159. Are there systems for recording and managing stocks (where part of contract)?

1160. Is it clear which procurement procedure your organization has opted for?

1161. Have late payment interests been rewarded and could they have been avoided?

1162. Are buyers rotated so that they do not deal with the same vendors year in and year out?

1163. Did the contracting authority verify compliance

with the basic requirements of the competition?

1164. Are receiving reports on file for all claims for equipment, supplies and materials in the paid claims file?

1165. How do you ensure whether the goods were supplied or works executed in time and properly recorded in measurement books and stock/works registers after inspection?

1166. Are the official minutes written in a clear and concise manner?

1167. What are the required standards of quality assurance or environmental management?

1168. Did the additional works introduce minor or non-substantial changes to performance, as described in the contract documents?

1169. Is there an effective risk management system continuously monitoring procurement risk?

1170. Was suitability of candidates accurately assessed?

1171. Has a deputy treasurer been appointed to sign checks when the treasurer is unable to perform that duty?

1172. Are there regular reviews and analysis of the performance of the procurement function/unit?

1173. Is there no evidence of unauthorized release of information or seemingly unnecessary contacts with bidders personnel during the evaluation and negotiation processes?

# 5.2 Contract Close-Out: MVNO

1174. Change in knowledge?

1175. Parties: who is involved?

1176. How does it work?

1177. How/when used ?

1178. How is the contracting office notified of the automatic contract close-out?

1179. Was the contract sufficiently clear so as not to result in numerous disputes and misunderstandings?

1180. What is capture management?

1181. Have all contract records been included in the MVNO project archives?

1182. Have all acceptance criteria been met prior to final payment to contractors?

1183. Are the signers the authorized officials?

1184. Change in attitude or behavior?

1185. Have all contracts been closed?

1186. Has each contract been audited to verify acceptance and delivery?

1187. Change in circumstances?

1188. Was the contract type appropriate?

1189. Have all contracts been completed?

1190. Parties: Authorized?

1191. Was the contract complete without requiring numerous changes and revisions?

1192. What happens to the recipient of services?

# 5.3 Project or Phase Close-Out: MVNO

1193. What stakeholder group needs, expectations, and interests are being met by the MVNO project?

1194. When and how were information needs best met?

1195. Who controlled key decisions that were made?

1196. Who controlled the resources for the MVNO project?

1197. What were the actual outcomes?

1198. Who are the MVNO project stakeholders and what are roles and involvement?

1199. Who exerted influence that has positively affected or negatively impacted the MVNO project?

1200. Is the lesson based on actual MVNO project experience rather than on independent research?

1201. Planned remaining costs?

1202. What are the marketing communication needs for each stakeholder?

1203. What are the informational communication needs for each stakeholder?

1204. If you were the MVNO project sponsor, how would you determine which MVNO project team(s) and/or individuals deserve recognition?

1205. Planned completion date?

1206. Have business partners been involved extensively, and what data was required for them?

1207. How often did each stakeholder need an update?

1208. Were messages directly related to the release strategy or phases of the MVNO project?

# 5.4 Lessons Learned: MVNO

1209. What were the main sources of frustration in the MVNO project?

1210. What worked well or did not work well, either for this MVNO project or for the MVNO project team?

1211. What is your overall assessment of the outcome of this MVNO project?

1212. What on the MVNO project worked well and was effective in the delivery of the product?

1213. How objective was the collection of data?

1214. What regulatory regime controlled how your organization head and program manager directed your organization and MVNO project?

1215. Was the necessary hardware, software, accommodation etc available?

1216. What was helpful to know when planning the deployment?

1217. Did the delivered product meet the specified requirements and goals of the MVNO project?

1218. How accurately and timely was the Risk Management Log updated or reviewed?

1219. Under what legal authority did your organization head and program manager direct your organization and MVNO project?

1220. What was the methodology behind successful learning experiences, and how might they be applied to the broader challenge of your organizations knowledge management?

1221. If you had to do this MVNO project again, what is the one thing that you would change (related to process, not to technical solutions)?

1222. How timely were Progress Reports provided to the MVNO project Manager by Team Members?

1223. Does the lesson describe a function that would be done differently the next time?

1224. Is the lesson significant, valid, and applicable?

1225. Overall, how effective were the efforts to prepare you and your organization for the impact of the product/service of the MVNO project?

1226. How effectively and timely was your organizational change impact identified and planned for?

1227. How well prepared were you to receive MVNO project deliverables?

1228. Are there any data that you have overlooked in identifying lessons?

# Index

management 1, 3-5, 9, 11-12, 19, 27-28, 31, 33, 71-73, 78, 97, 99, 106, 124-126, 136-137, 139-141, 143, 149-150, 152, 157-158, 168, 170-172, 174, 176, 178, 182, 184, 189-191, 194, 196, 198, 200-201, 208, 211-214, 216, 218-219, 225-227, 230, 232, 235, 239, 245, 247, 251-252, 256, 258, 262-263

CPSIA information can be obtained
at www.ICGtesting.com
Printed in the USA
BVHW080802220419
546159BV00025B/1720/P